Coloring for the Rest of Us

ANGELS

From Vintage to Modern

By The Literate Phoenix and the Quizzical Gryphon Productions

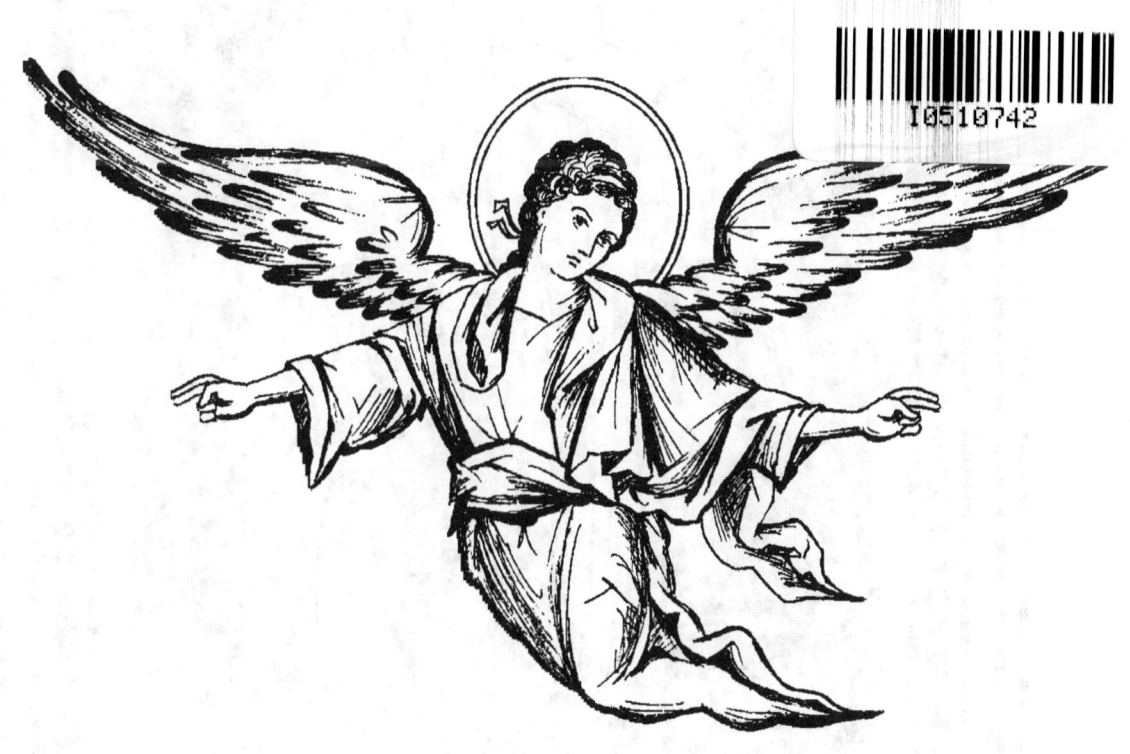

Angels Adult Coloring Book

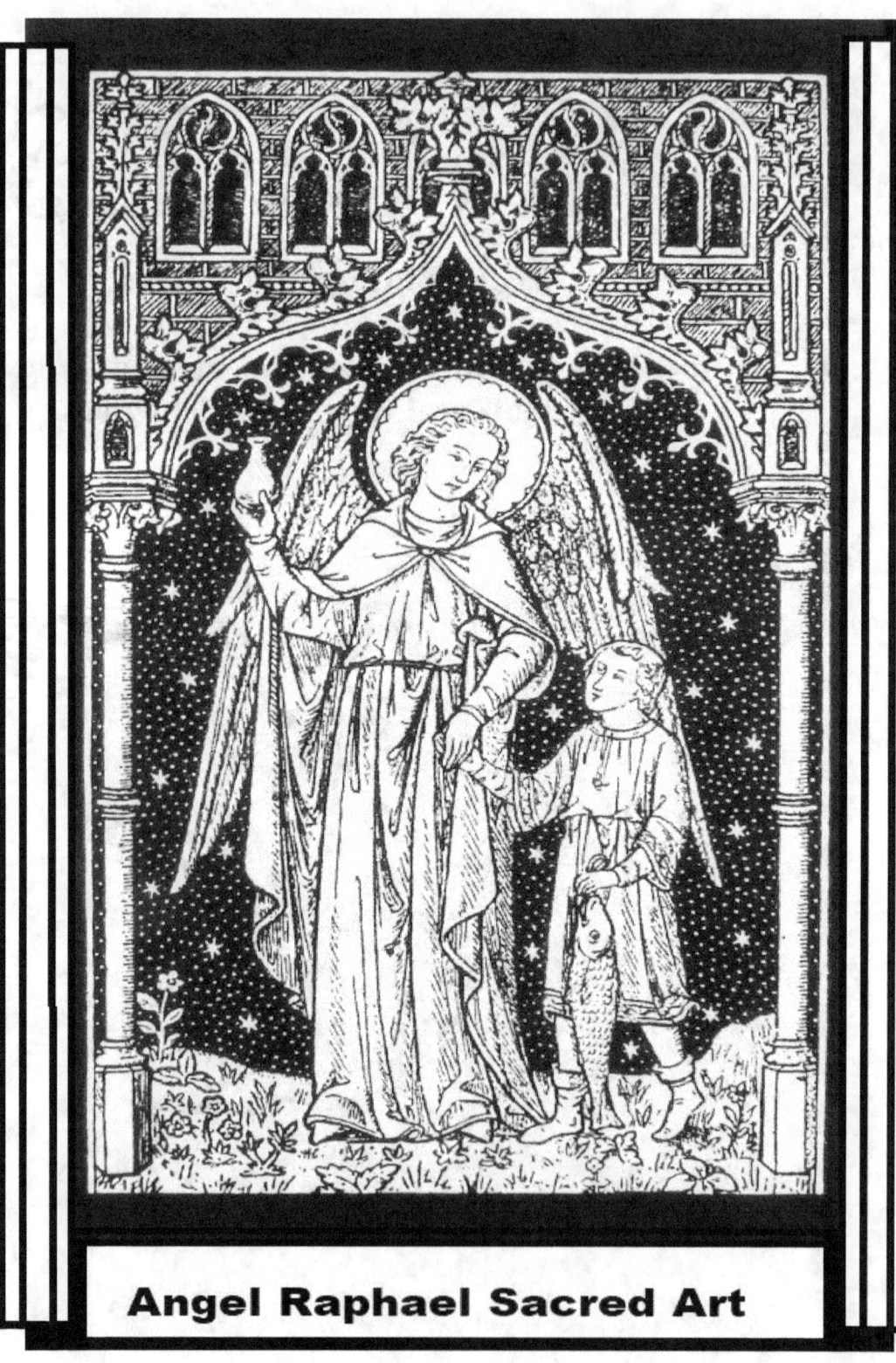

Angel Raphael Sacred Art

Angels Adult Coloring Book

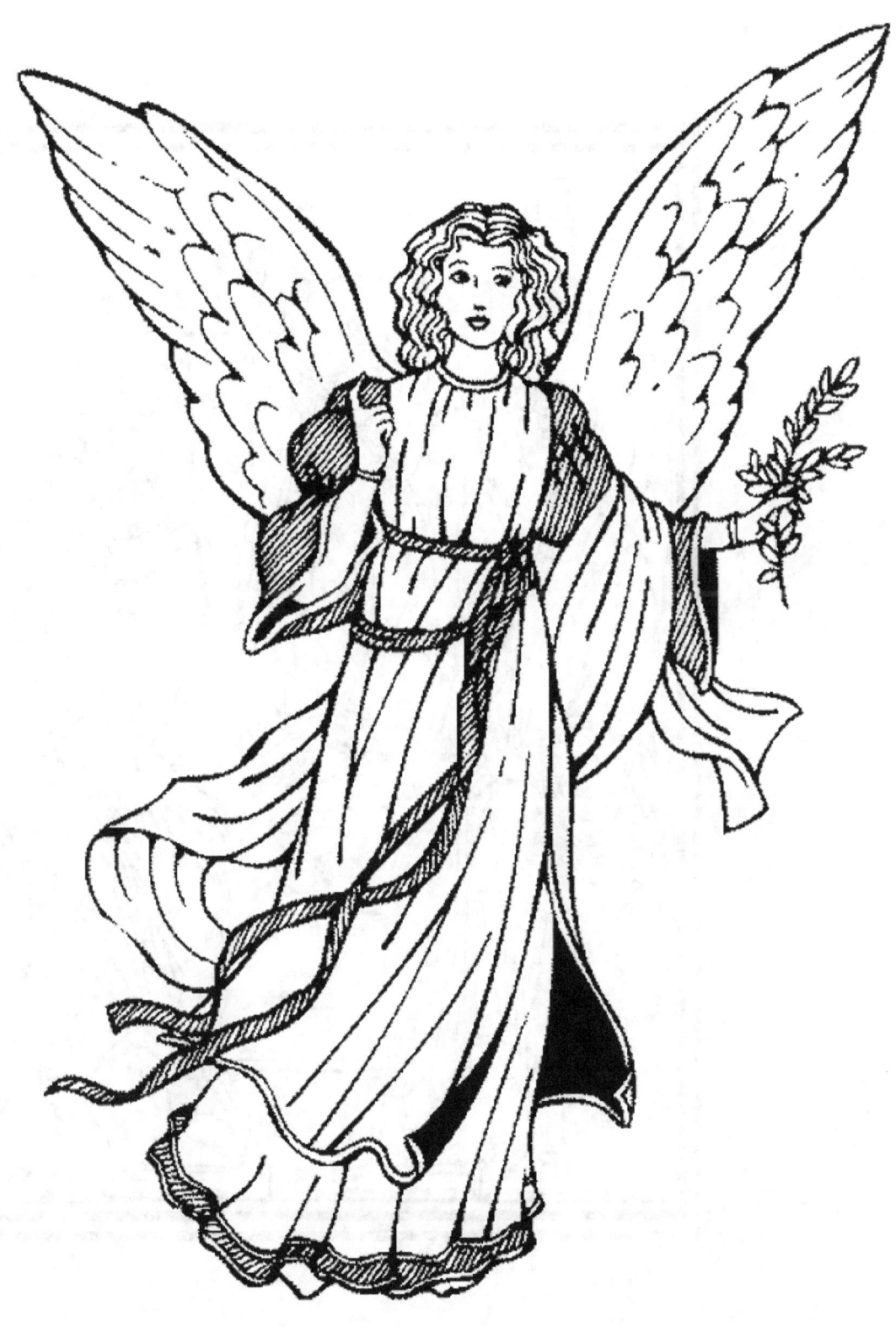

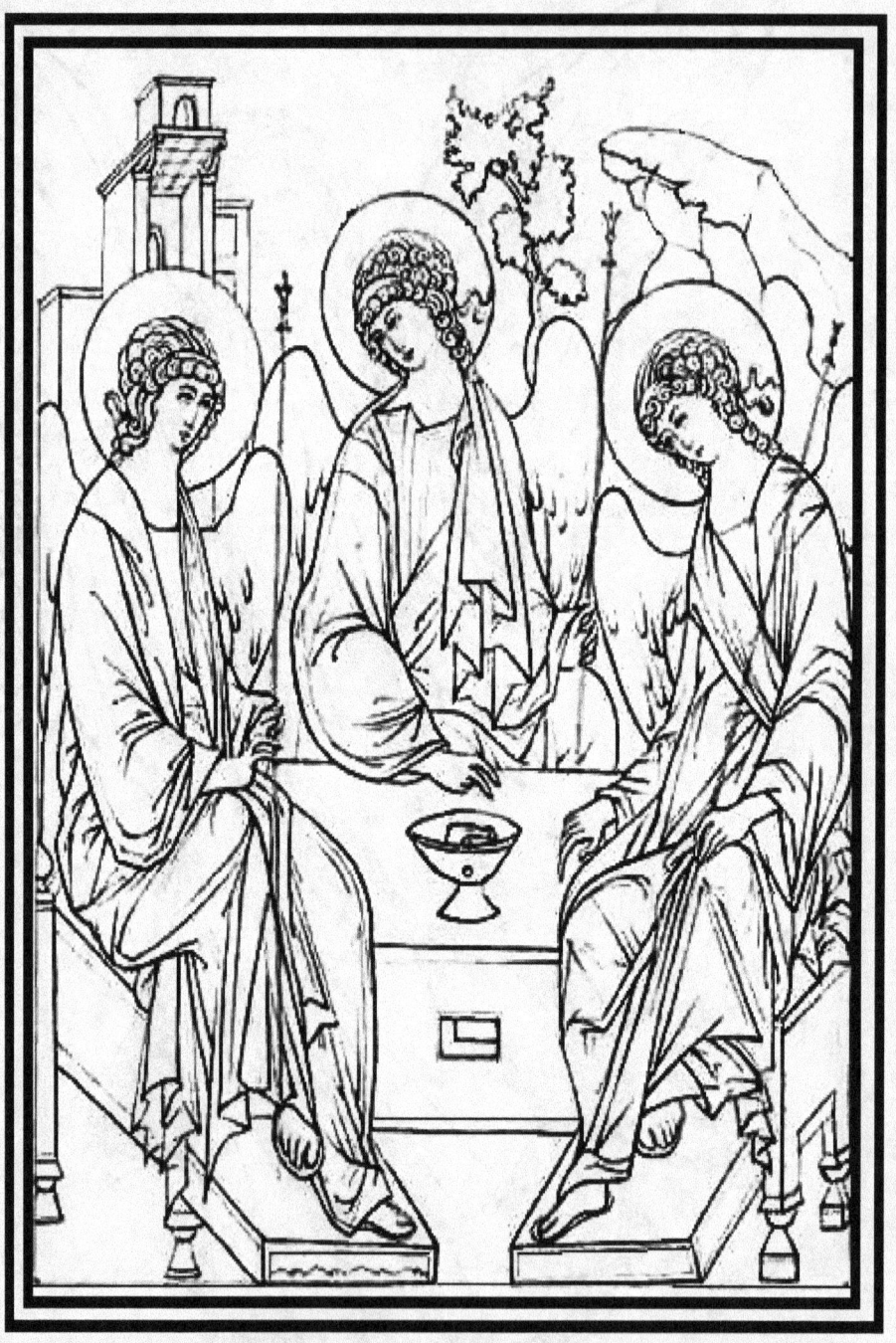

Angels Adult Coloring Book

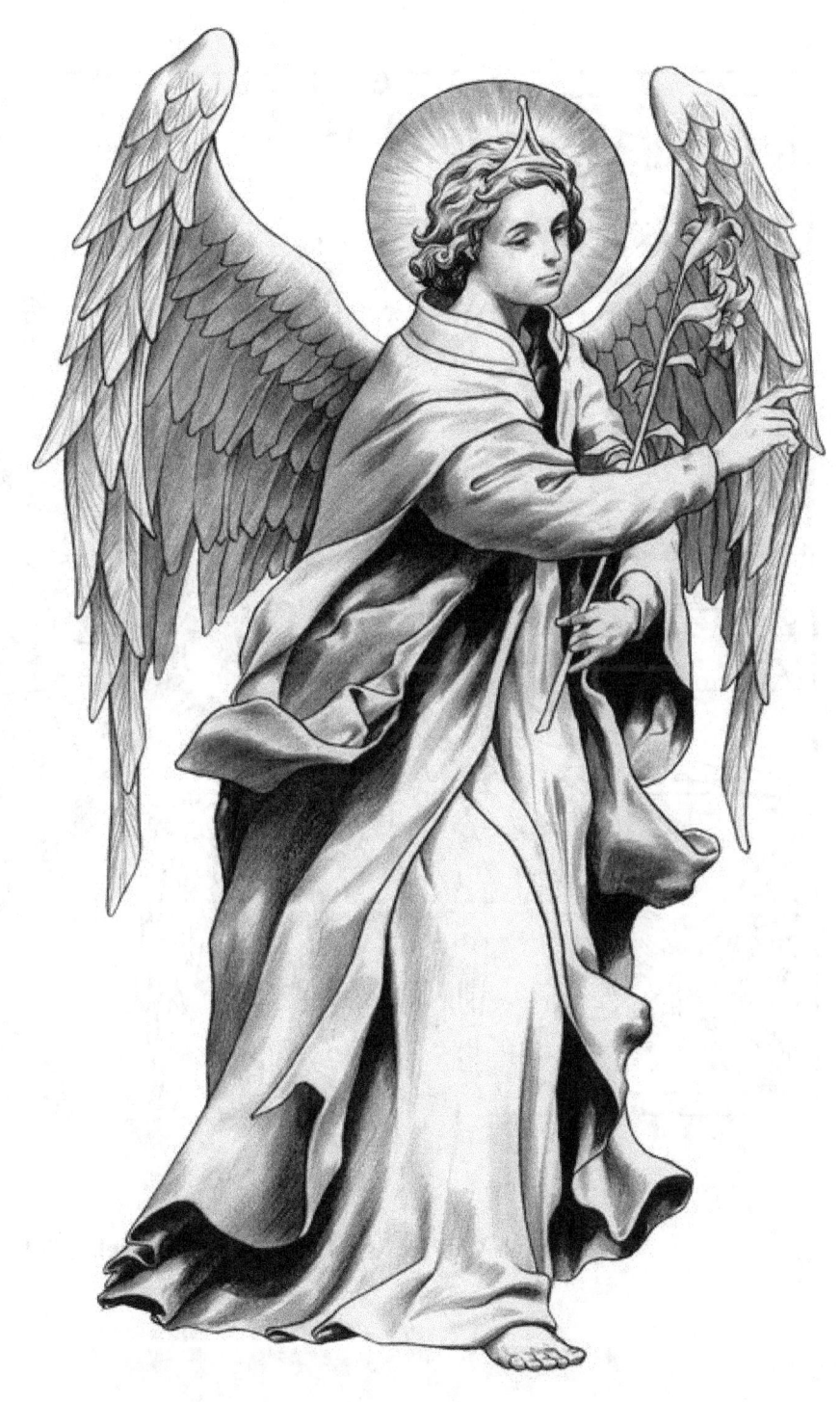

Angels Adult Coloring Book

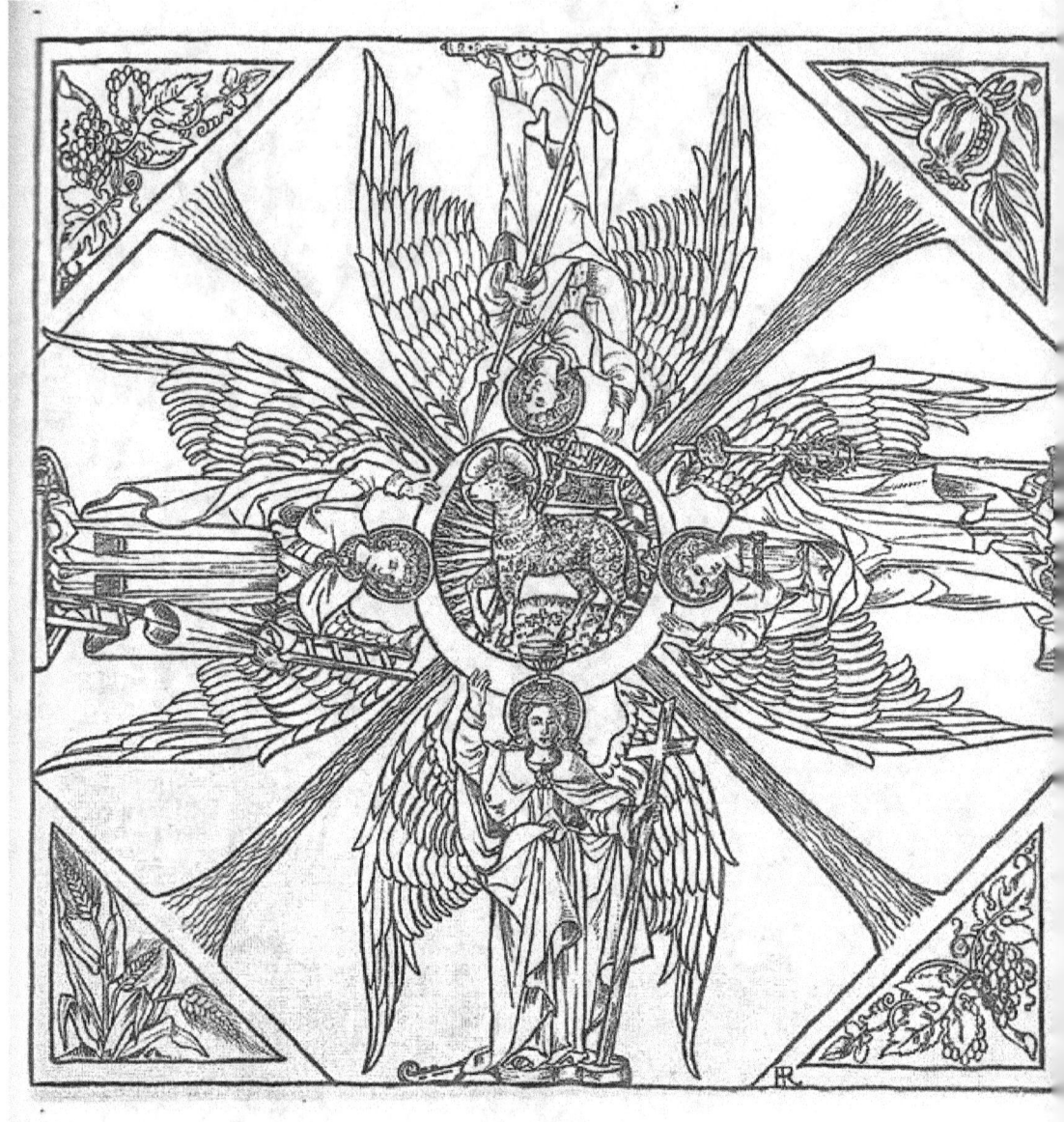

Chalice Veil Design from Alethea Wiel, 1894

Angels Adult Coloring Book

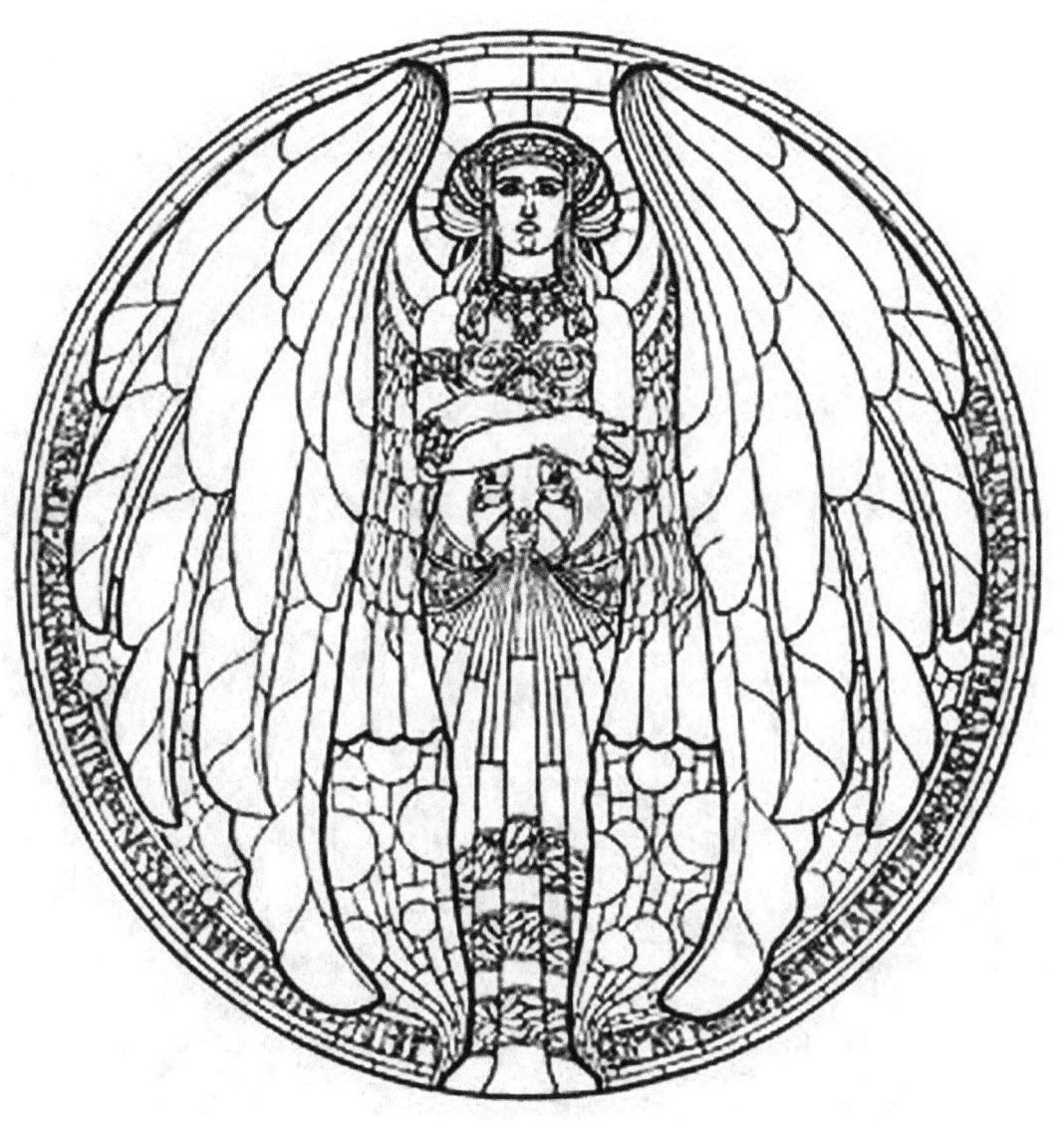

Angels Adult Coloring Book

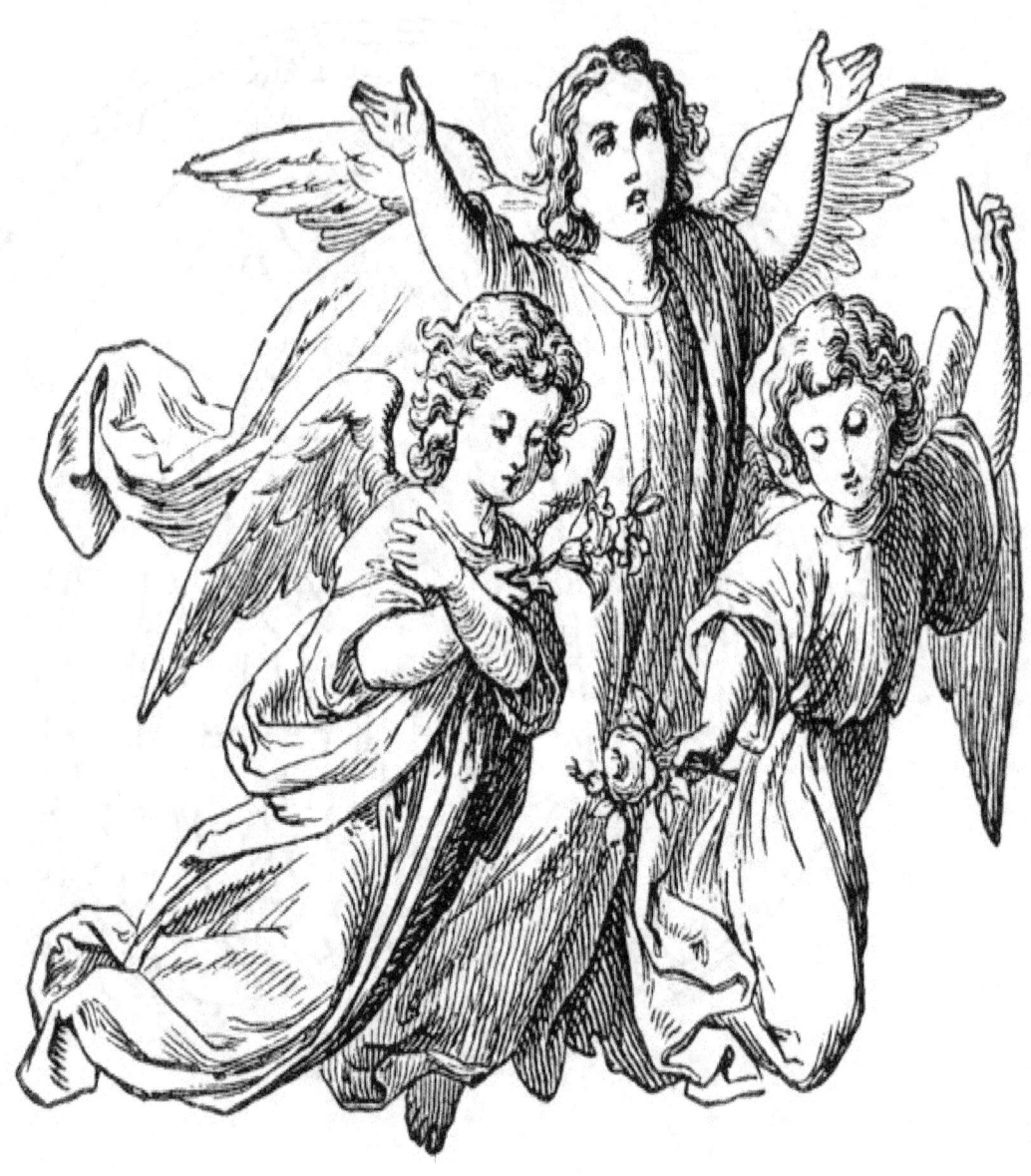

Angels Adult Coloring Book

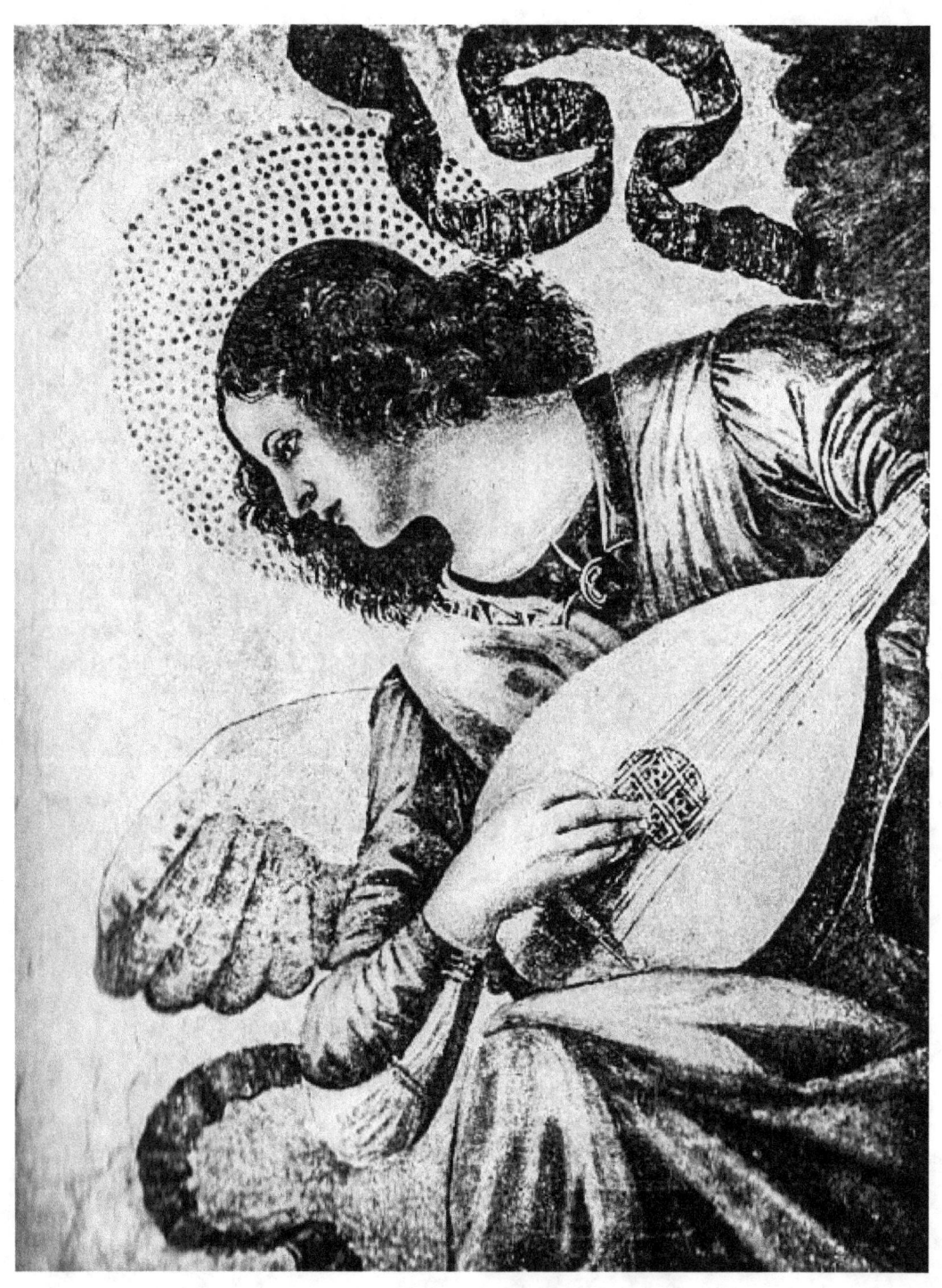

Angels Adult Coloring Book

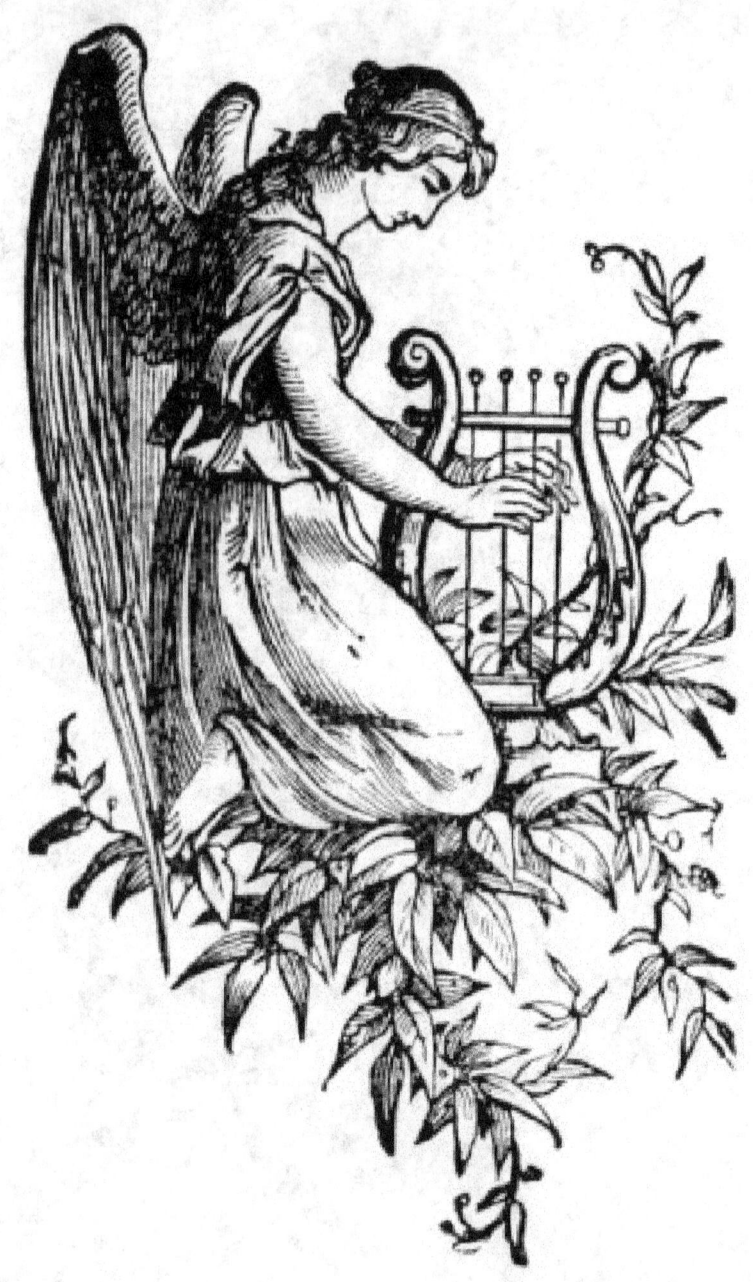

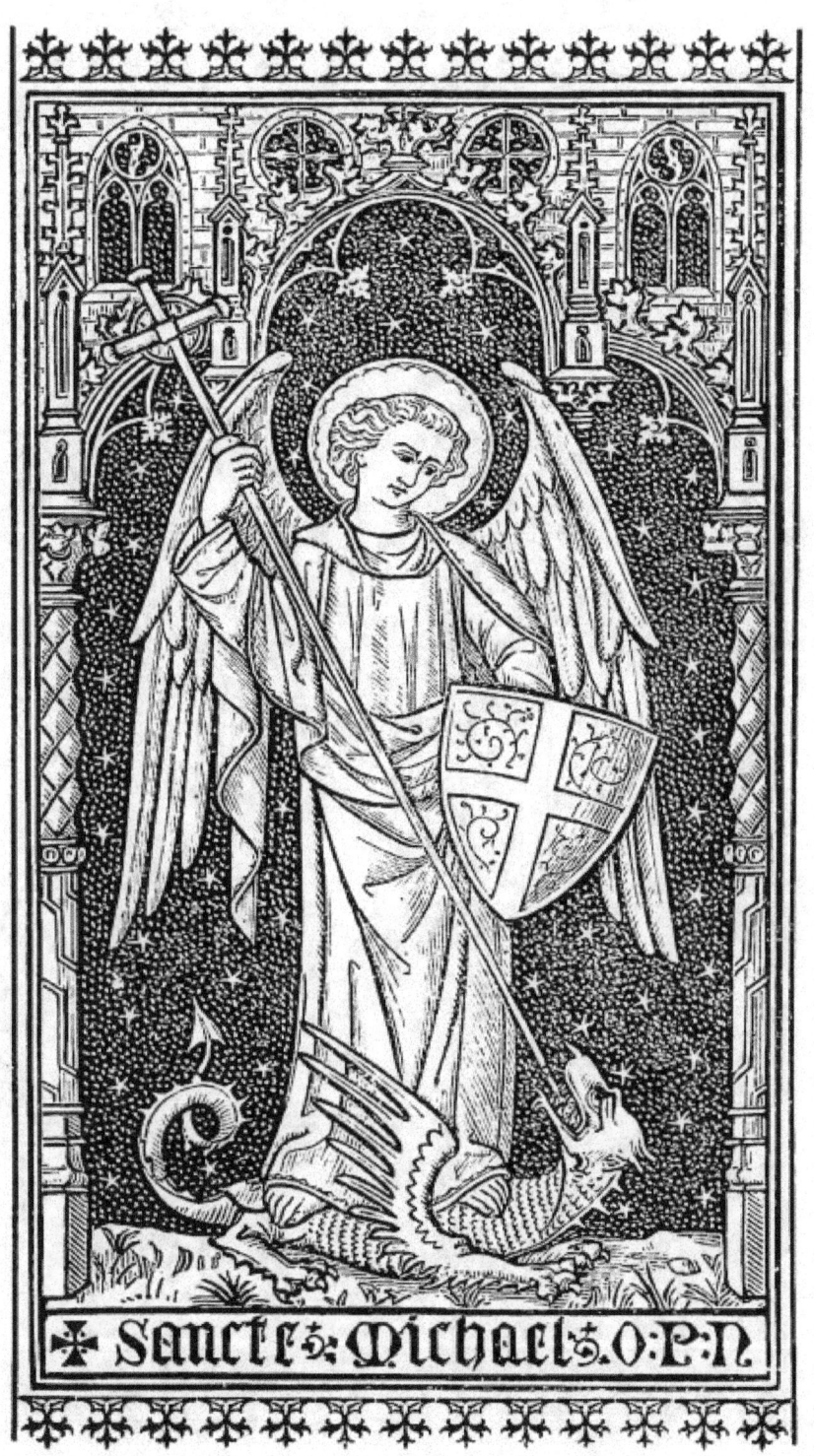

Angels Adult Coloring Book

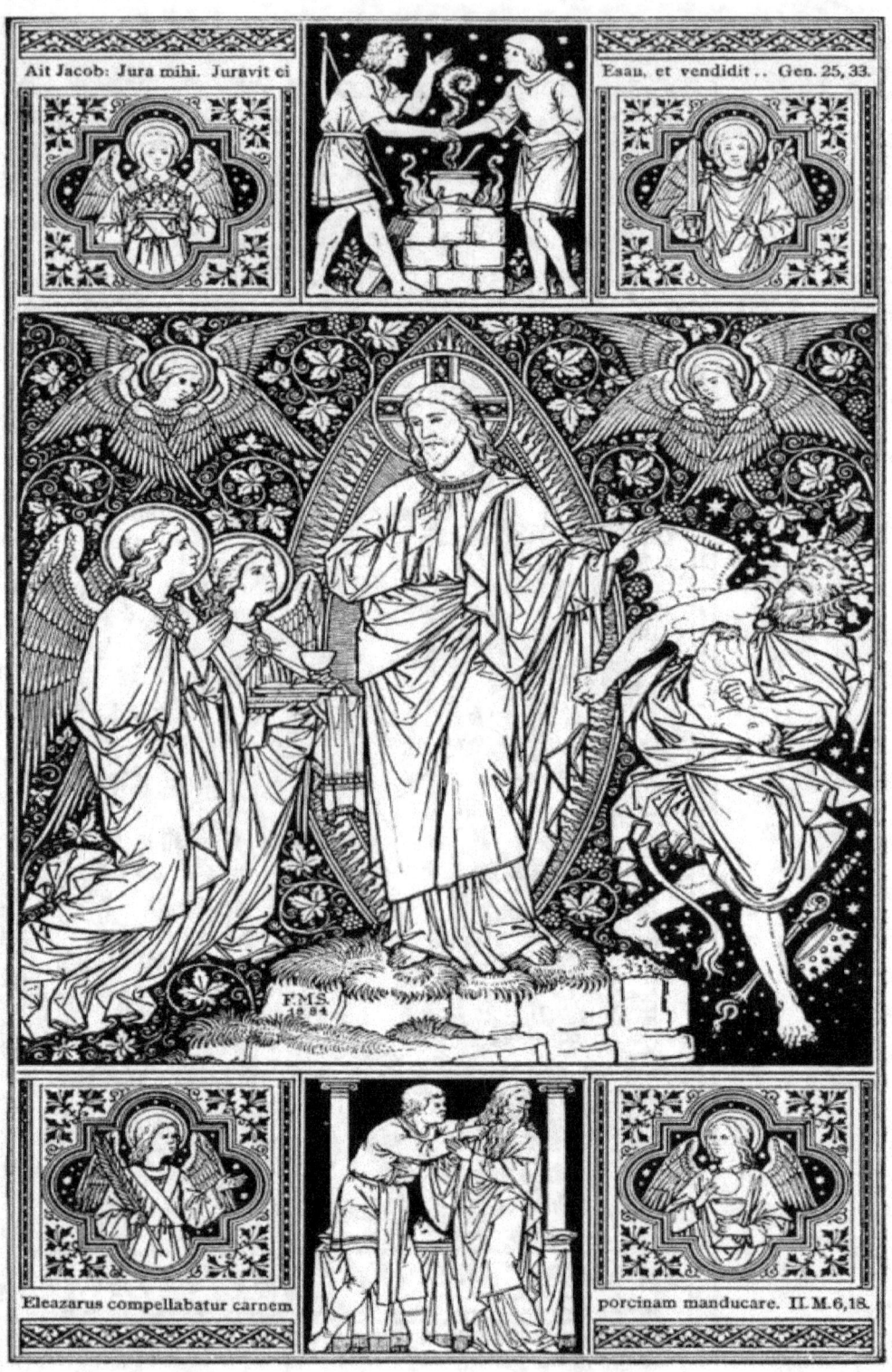

Angels Adult Coloring Book

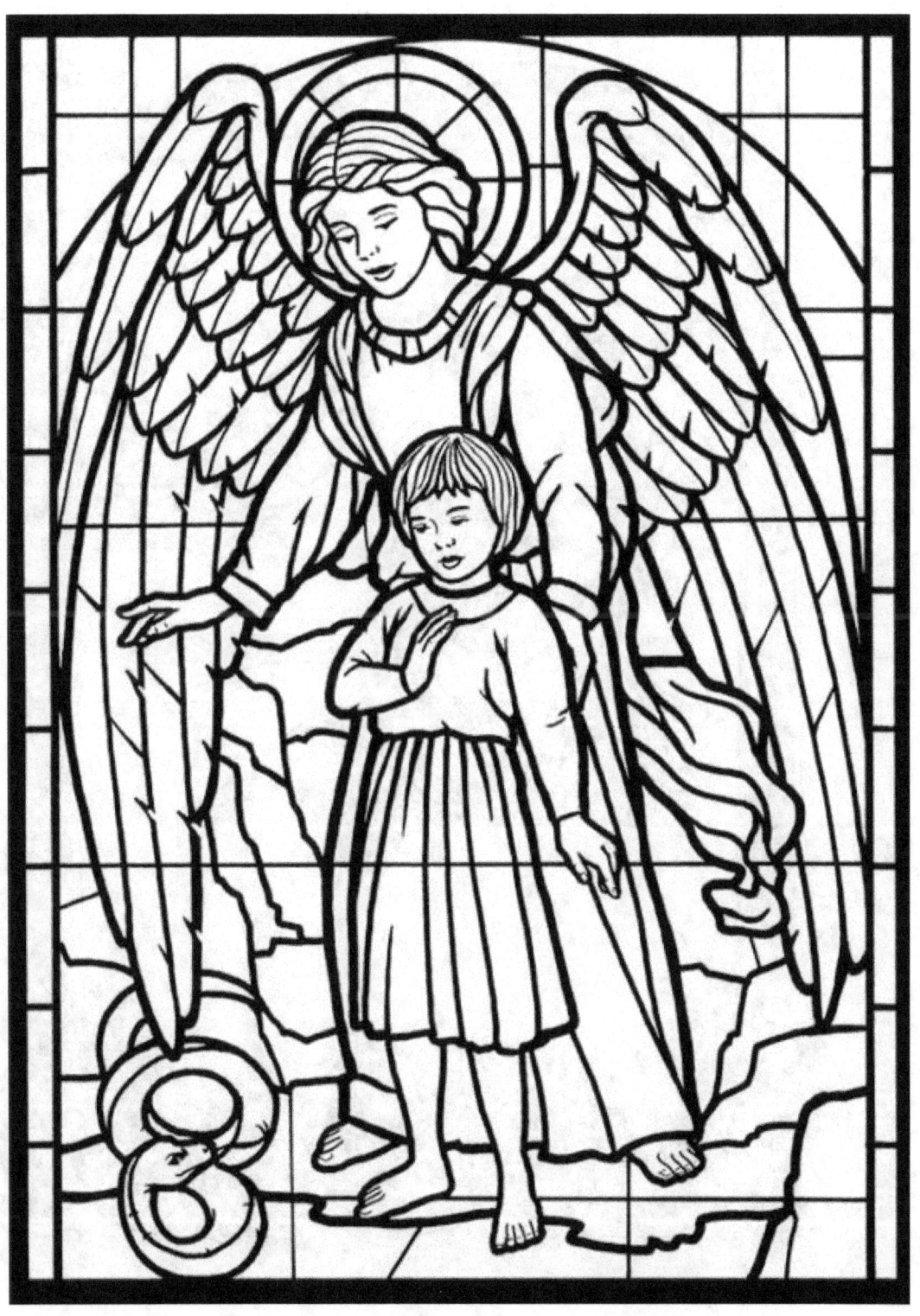

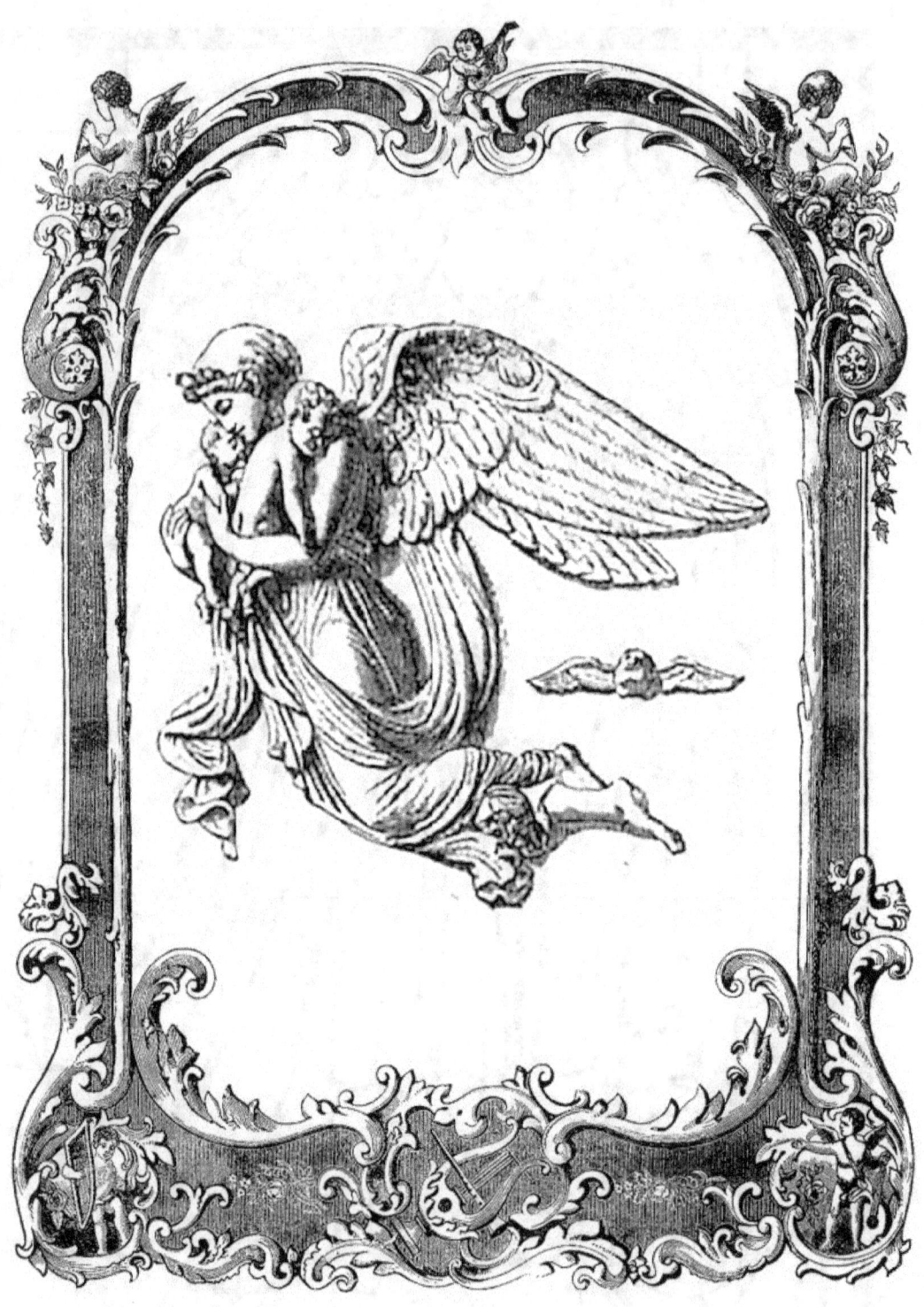

Angels Adult Coloring Book

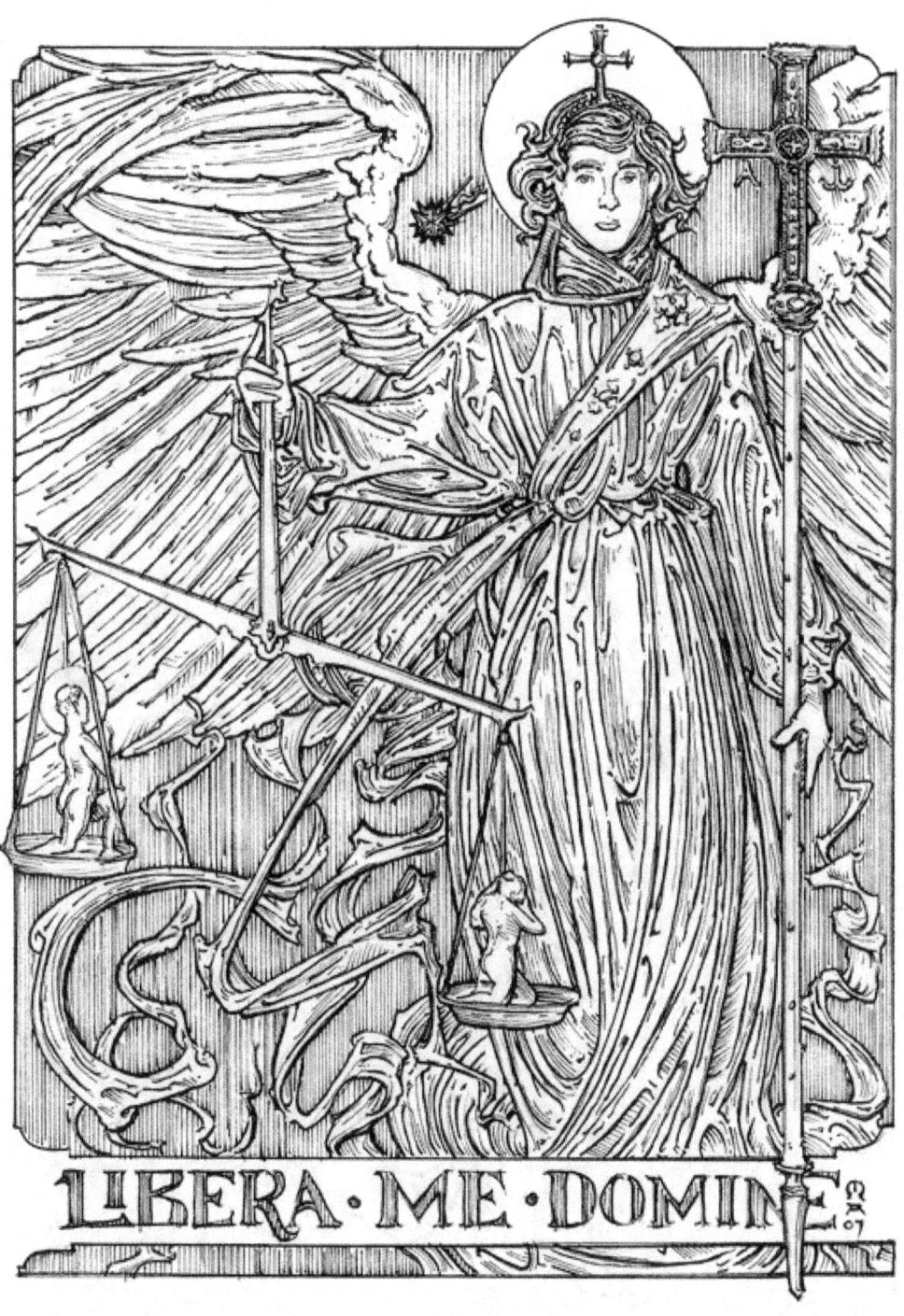

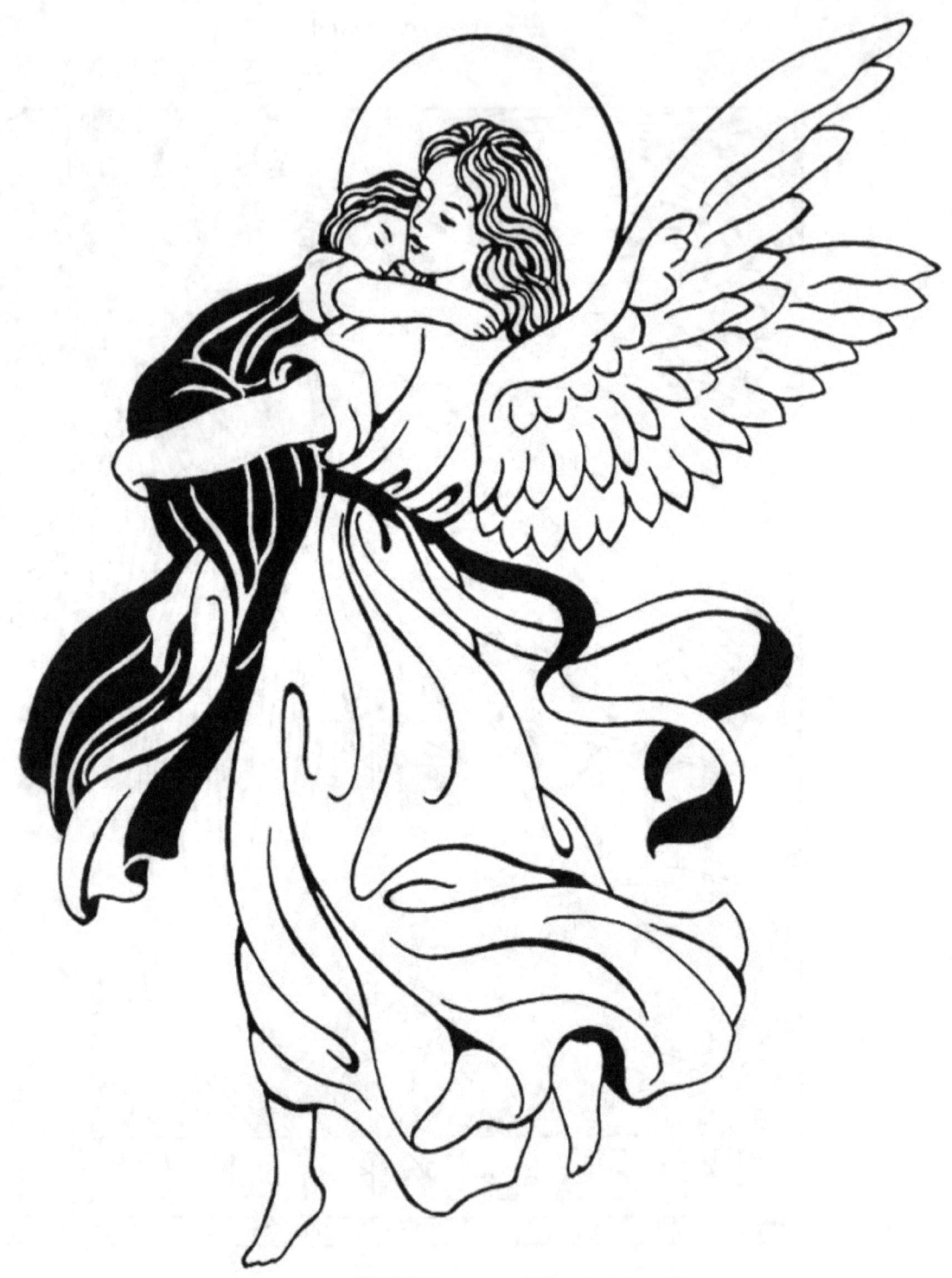

Child Protected by An Angel

Angels Adult Coloring Book

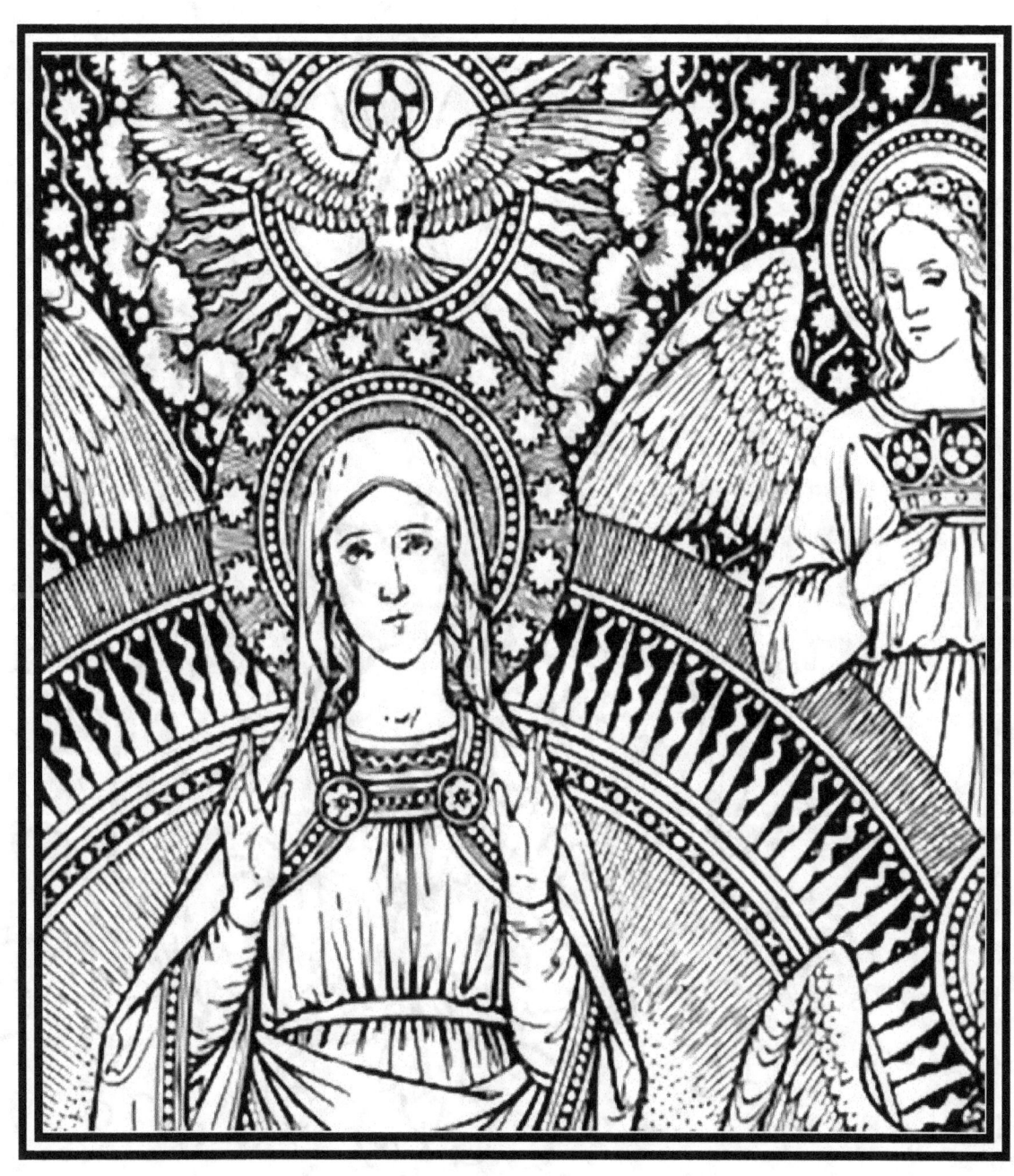

Mary with Angels and the Holy Spirit

Angels Adult Coloring Book

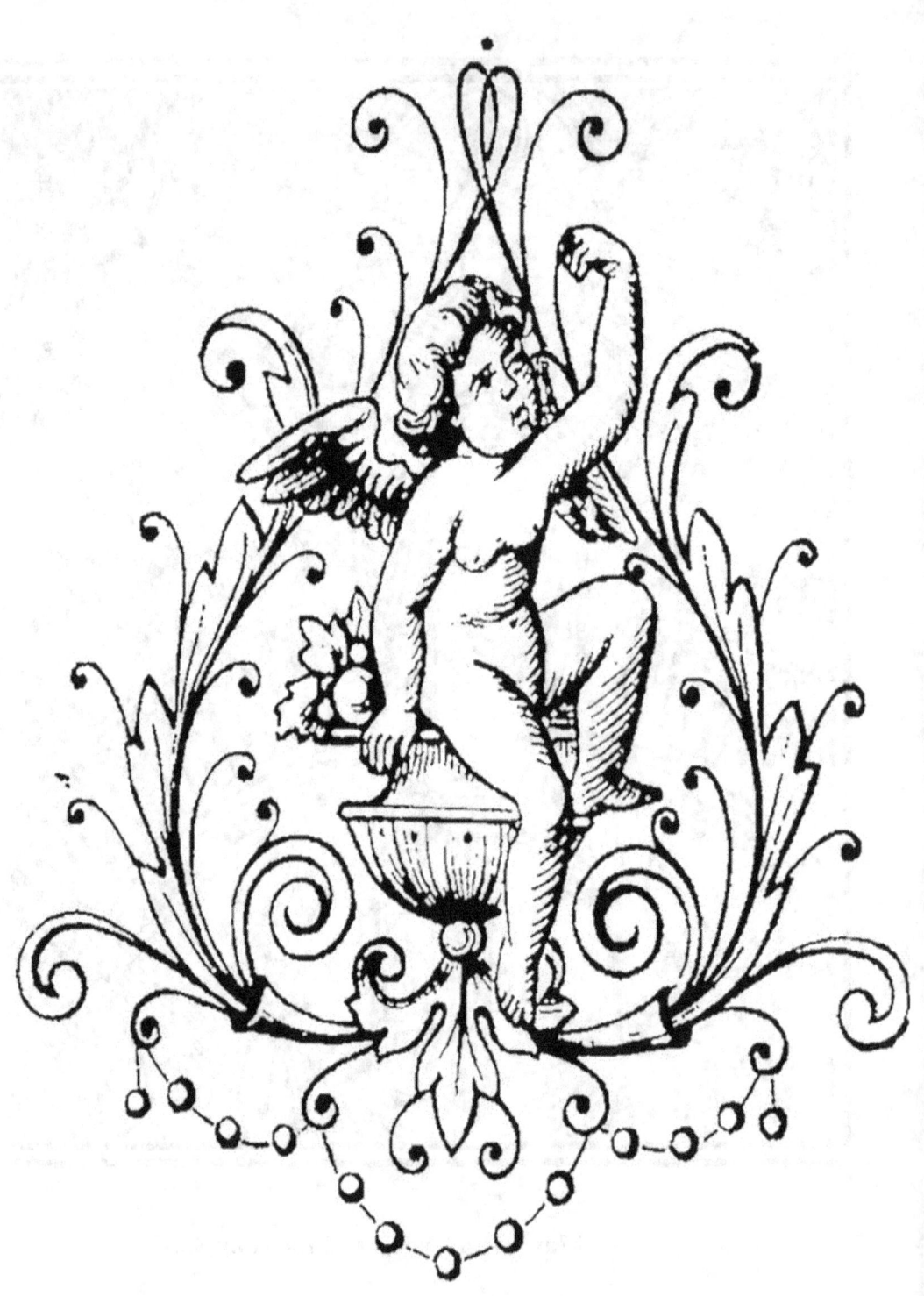

Angels Adult Coloring Book

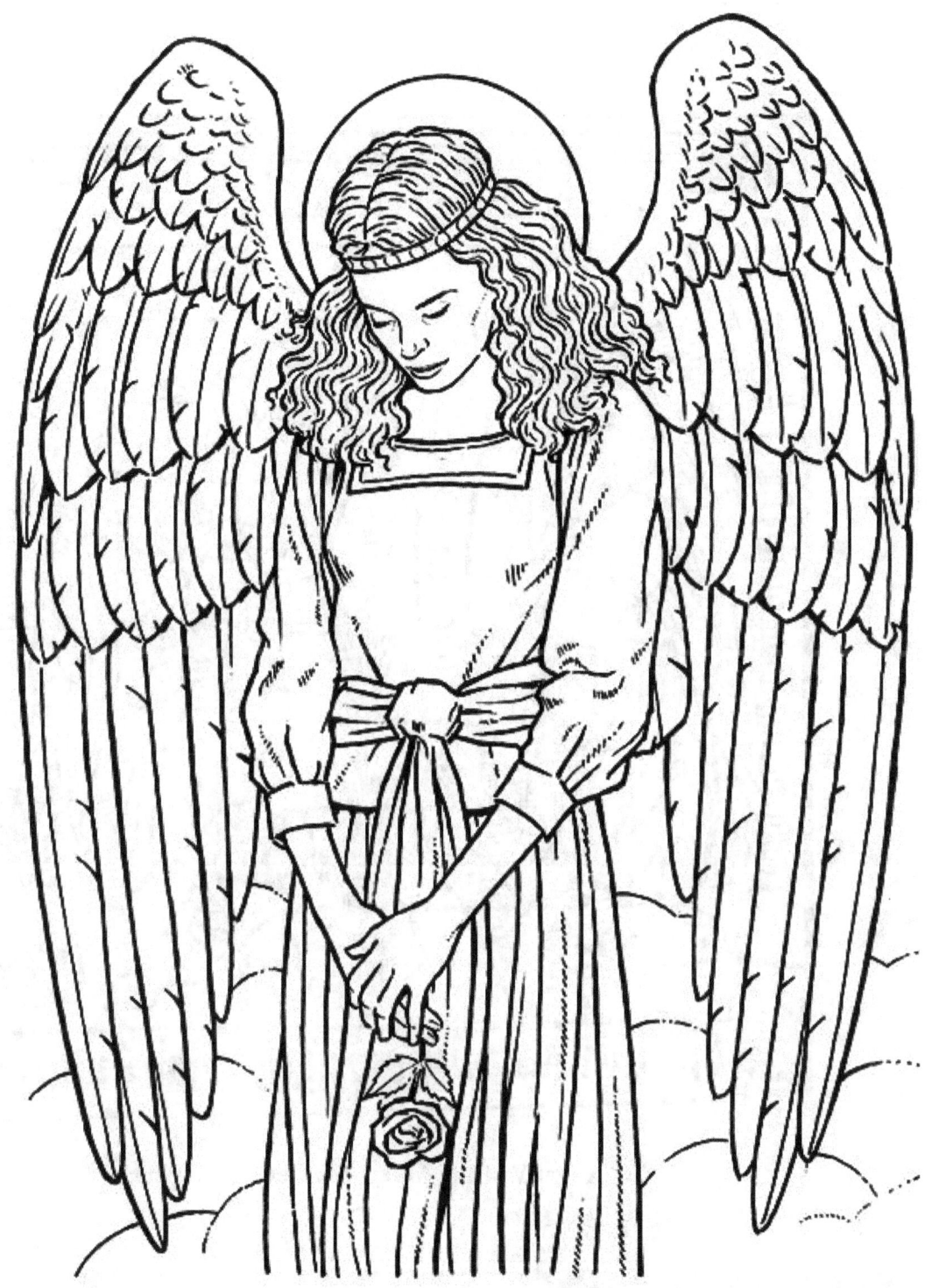

Eloa, Angel of Compassion

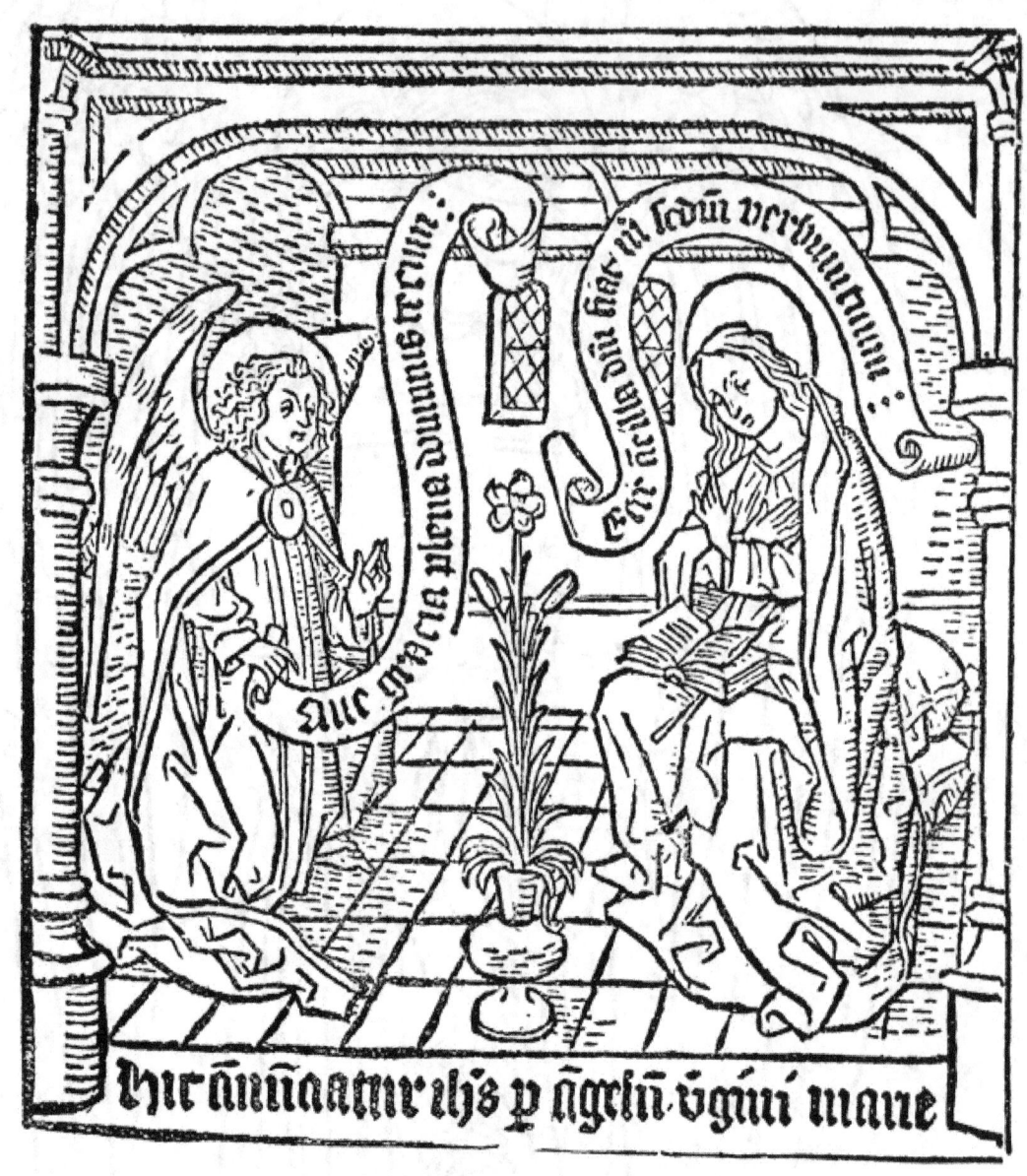

Angel Visiting Mary -Medieval Drawing

Angels Adult Coloring Book

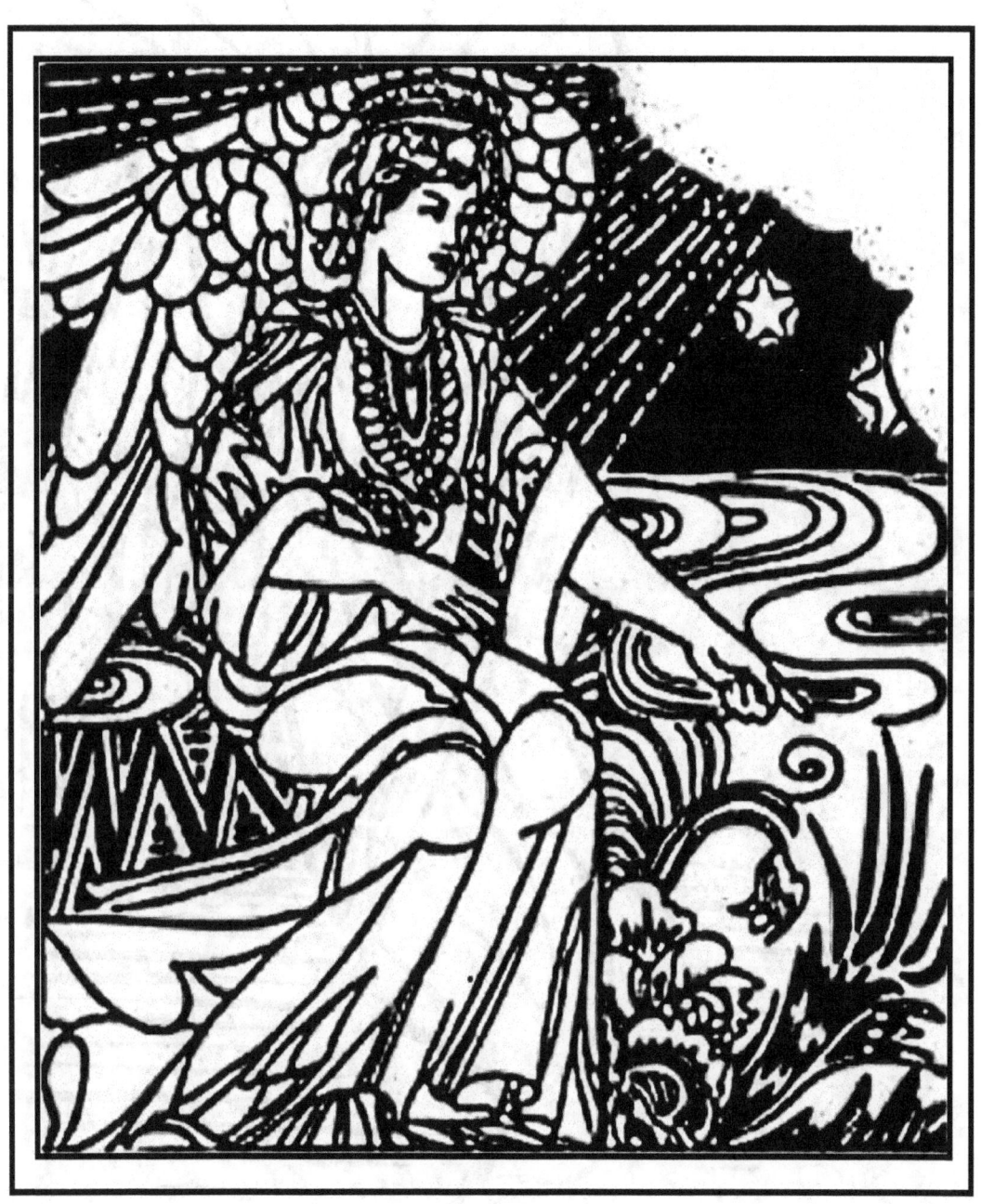

Angels Adult Coloring Book

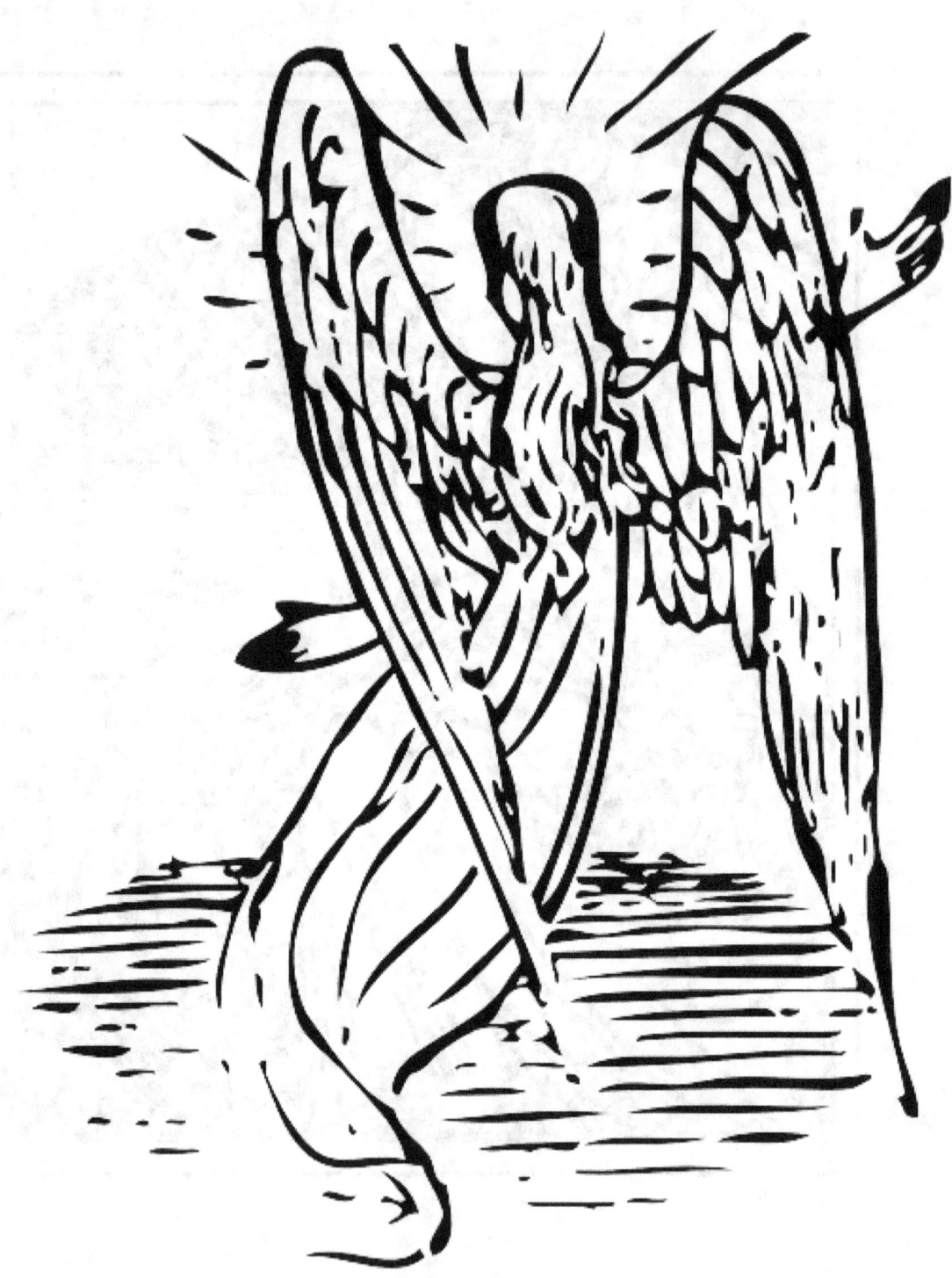

Angels Adult Coloring Book

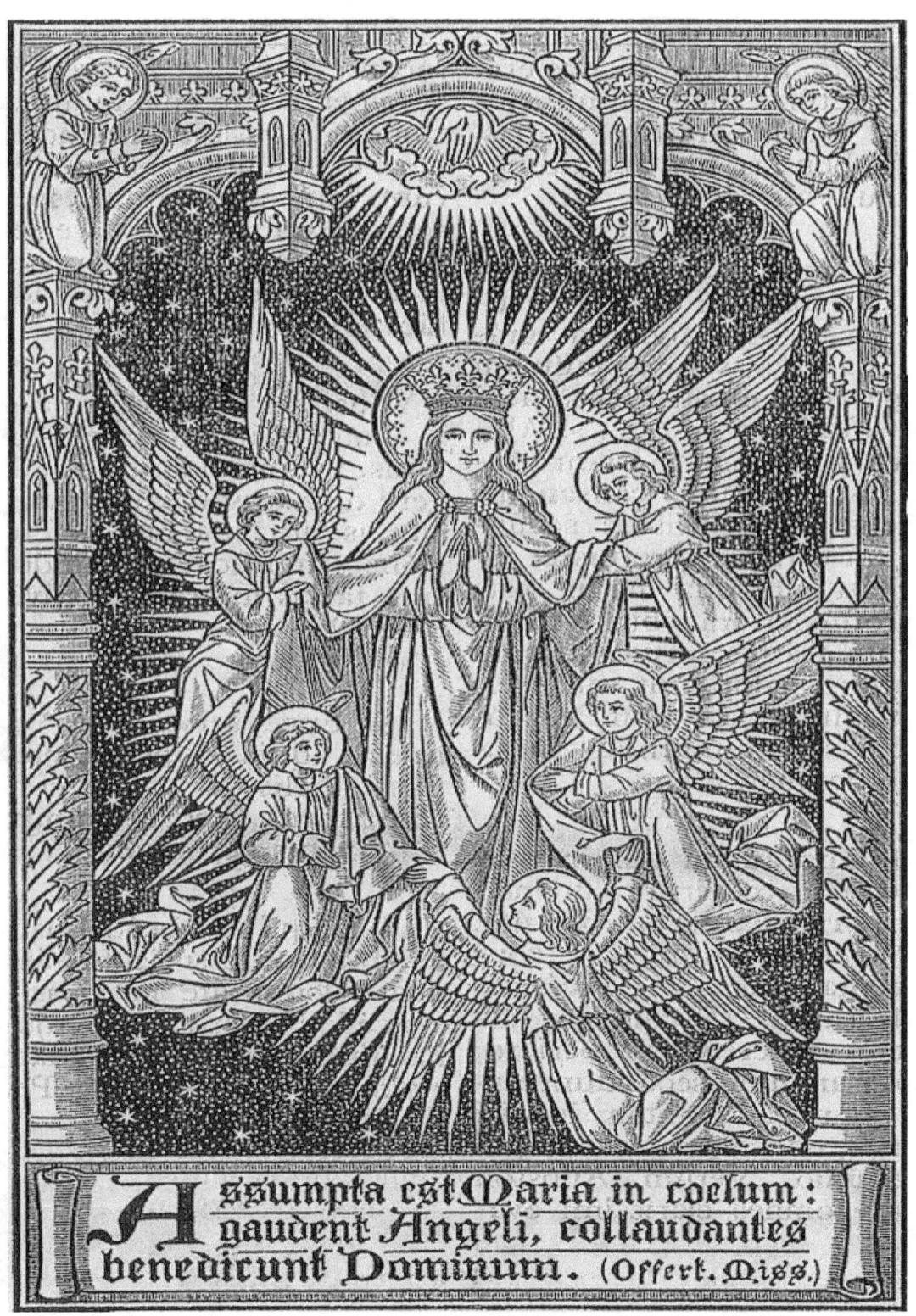

Assumpta est Maria in coelum: gaudent Angeli, collaudantes benedicunt Dominum. (Offert. Miss.)

Angels Adult Coloring Book

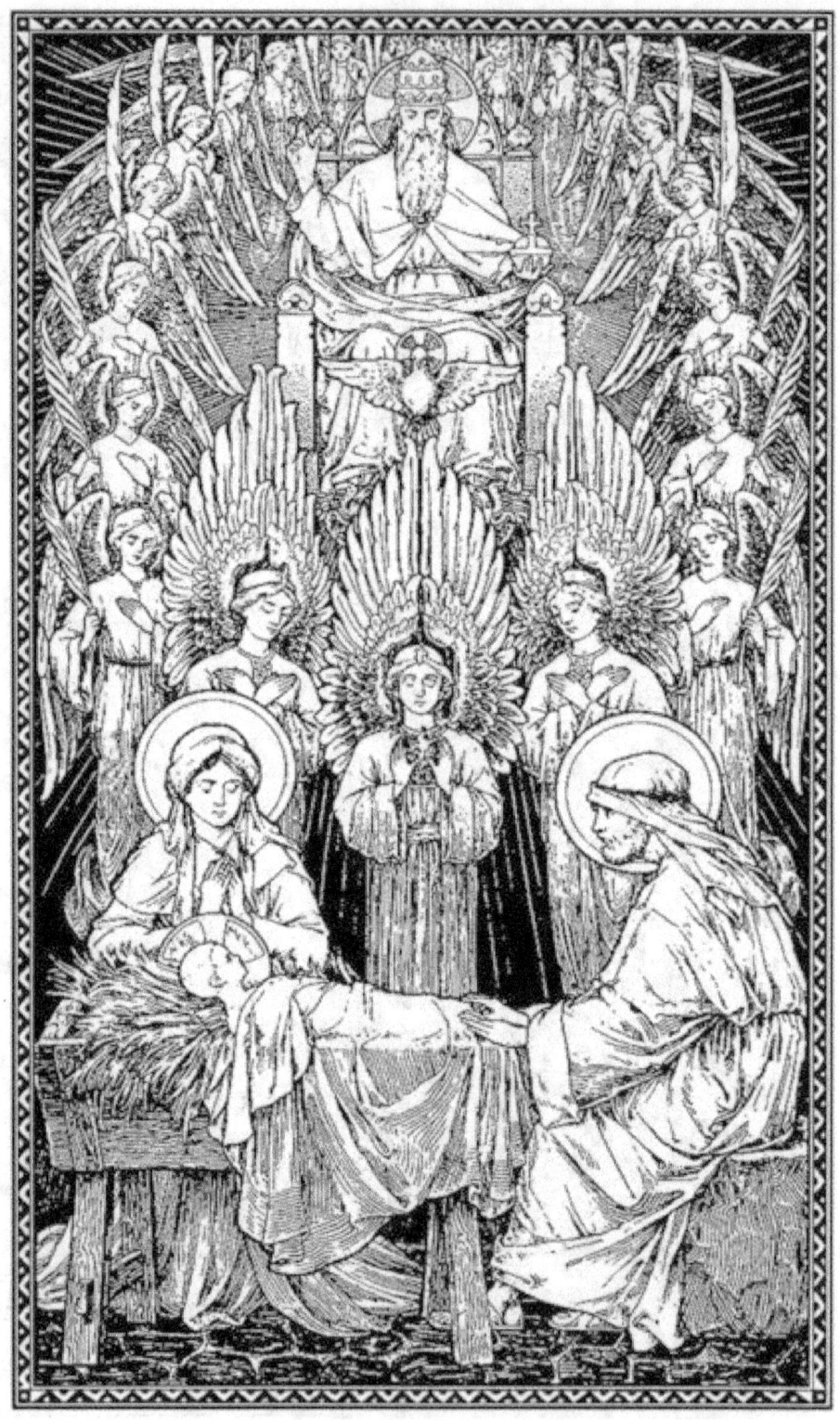

Angels Adult Coloring Book

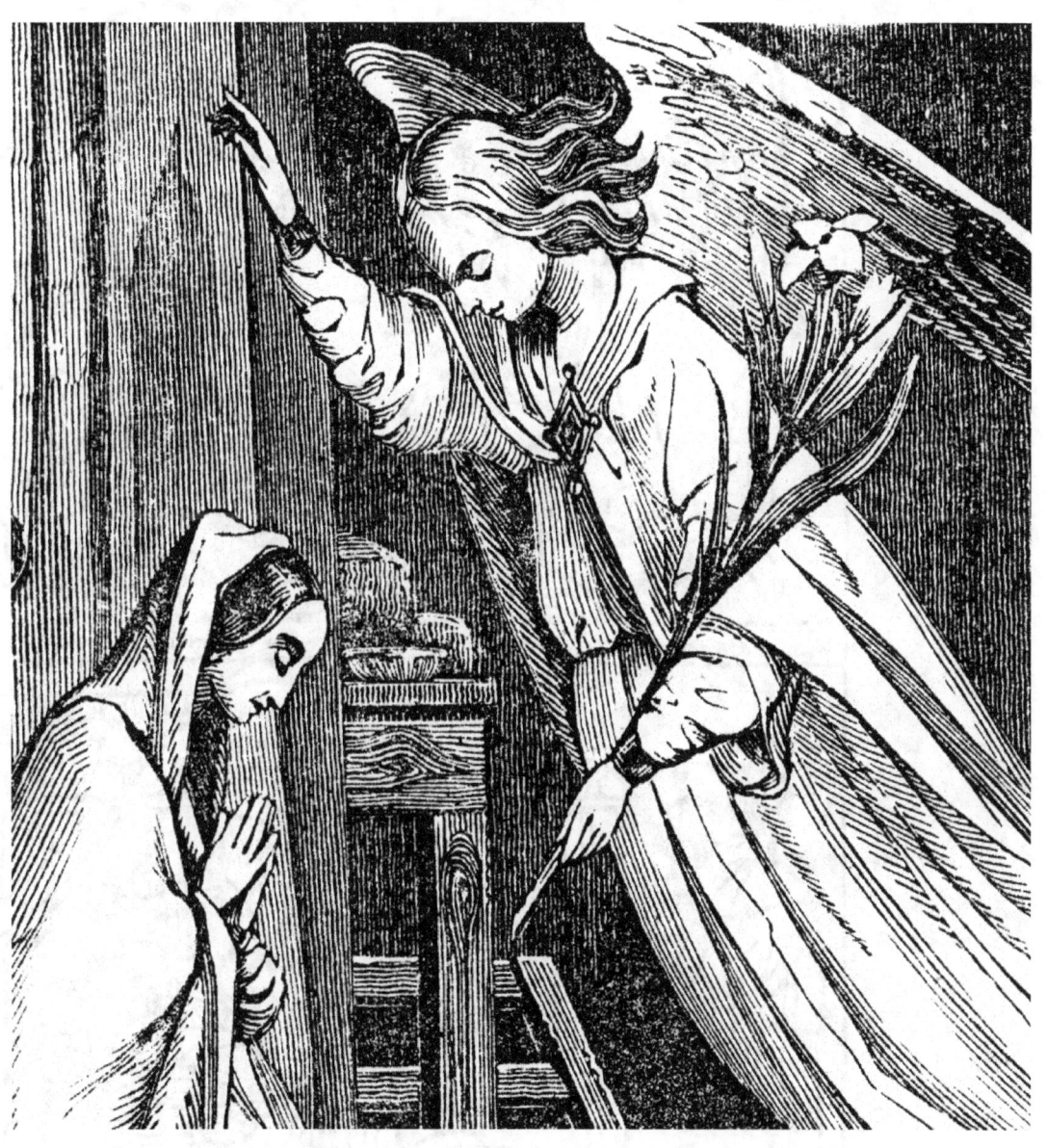

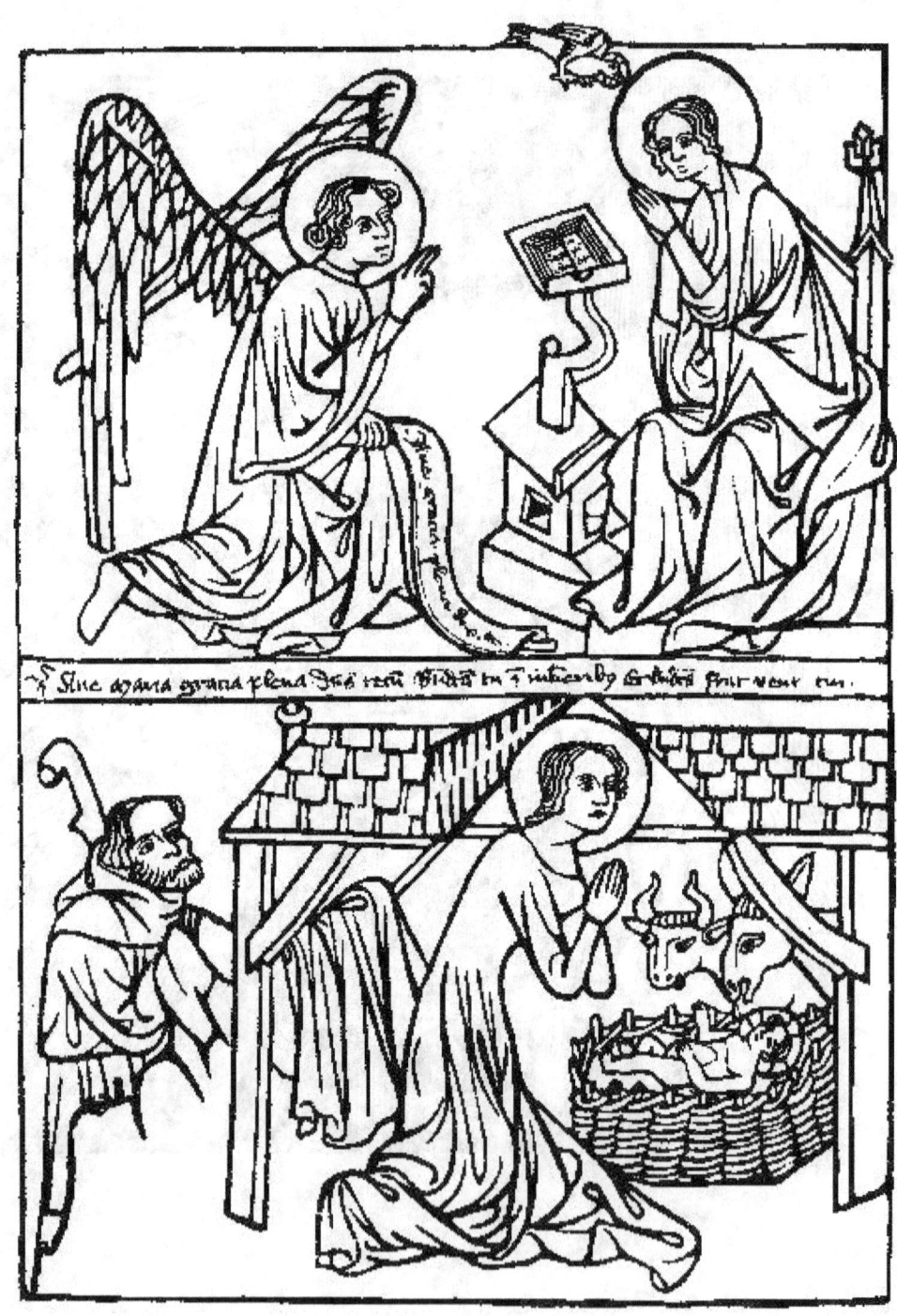

Angels Adult Coloring Book

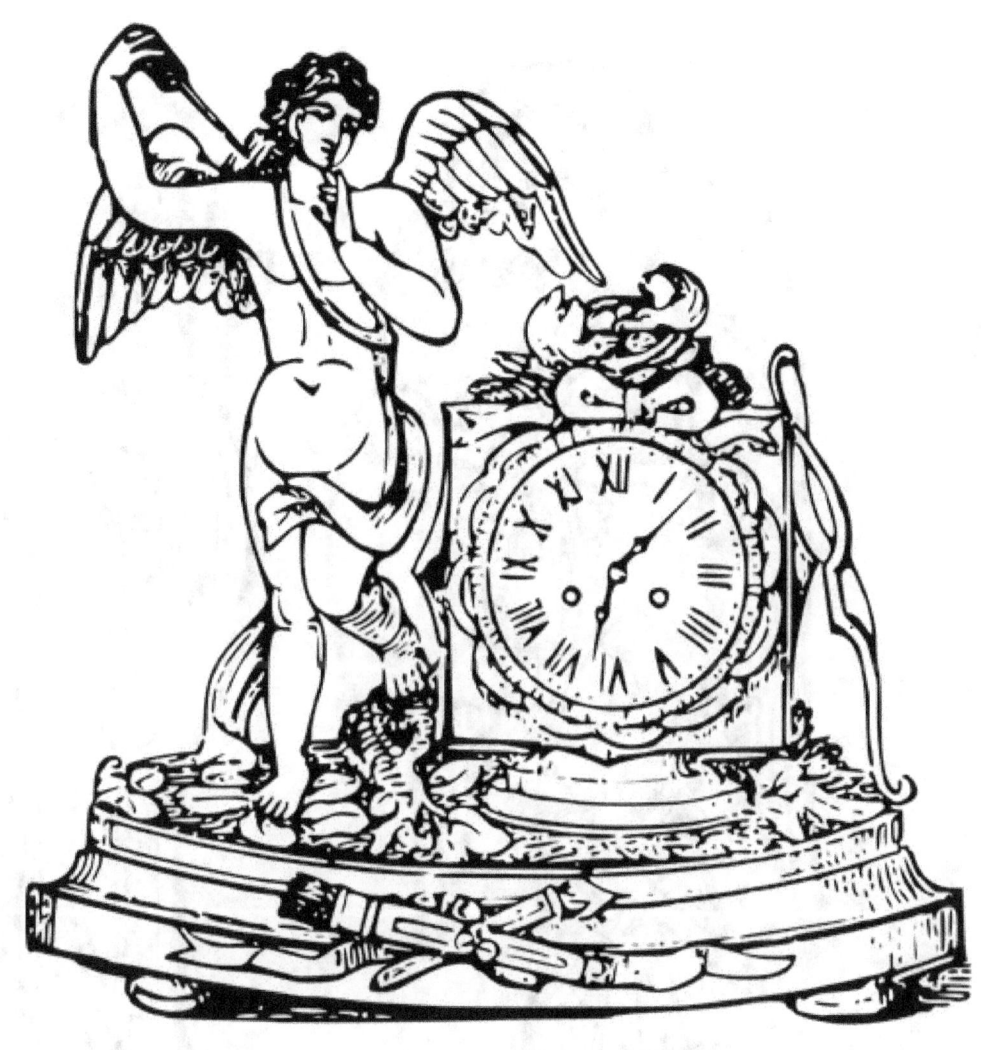

Art Deco Angel Clock

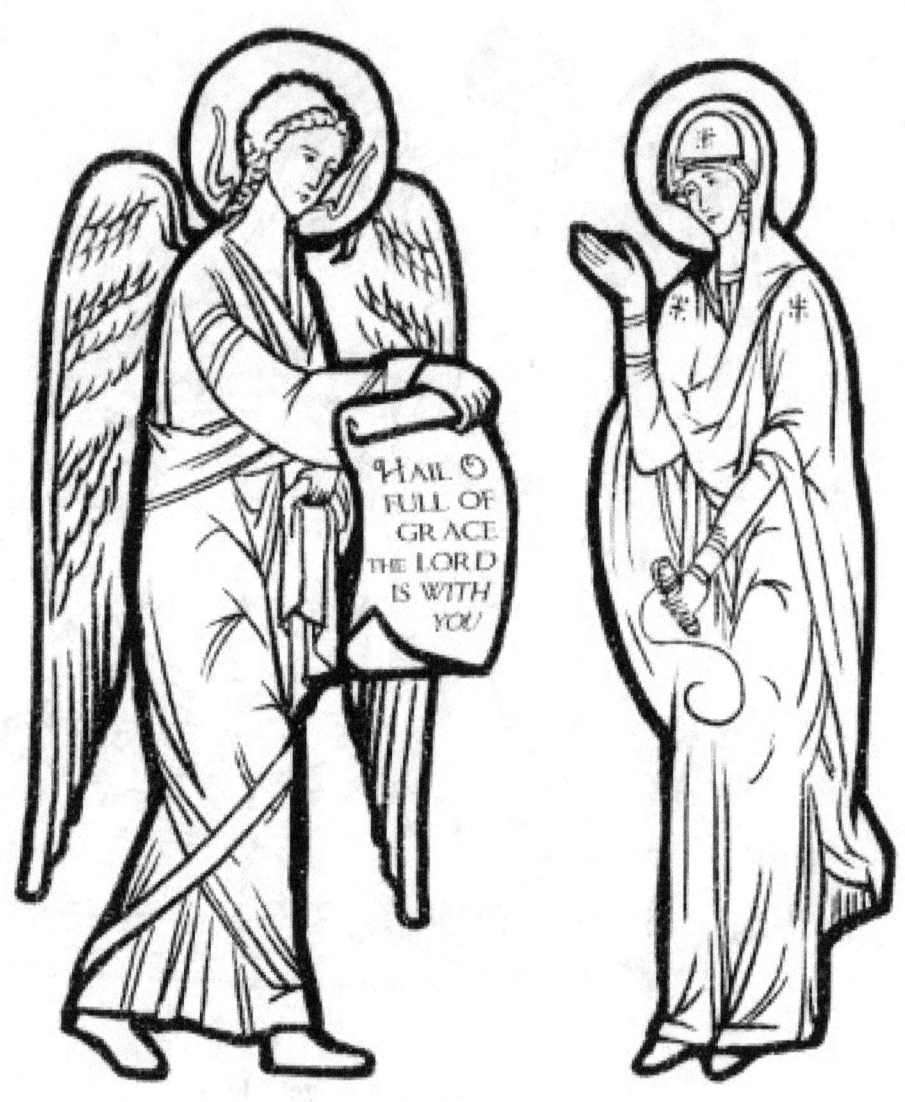

Within the illustration, on the scroll held by the angel:

HAIL ⊙
FULL OF
GRACE
THE LORD
IS WITH
YOU

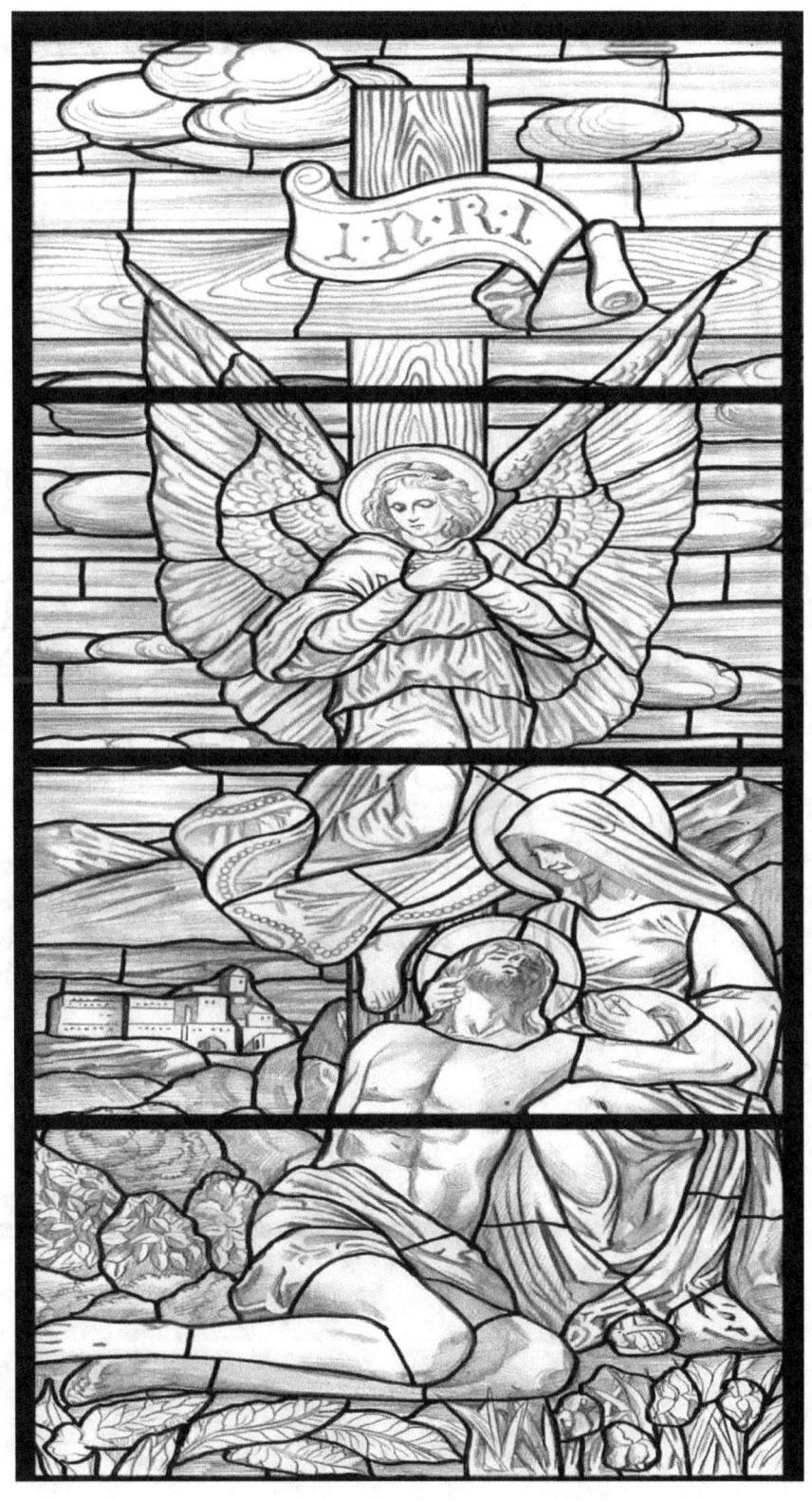

Angels Adult Coloring Book

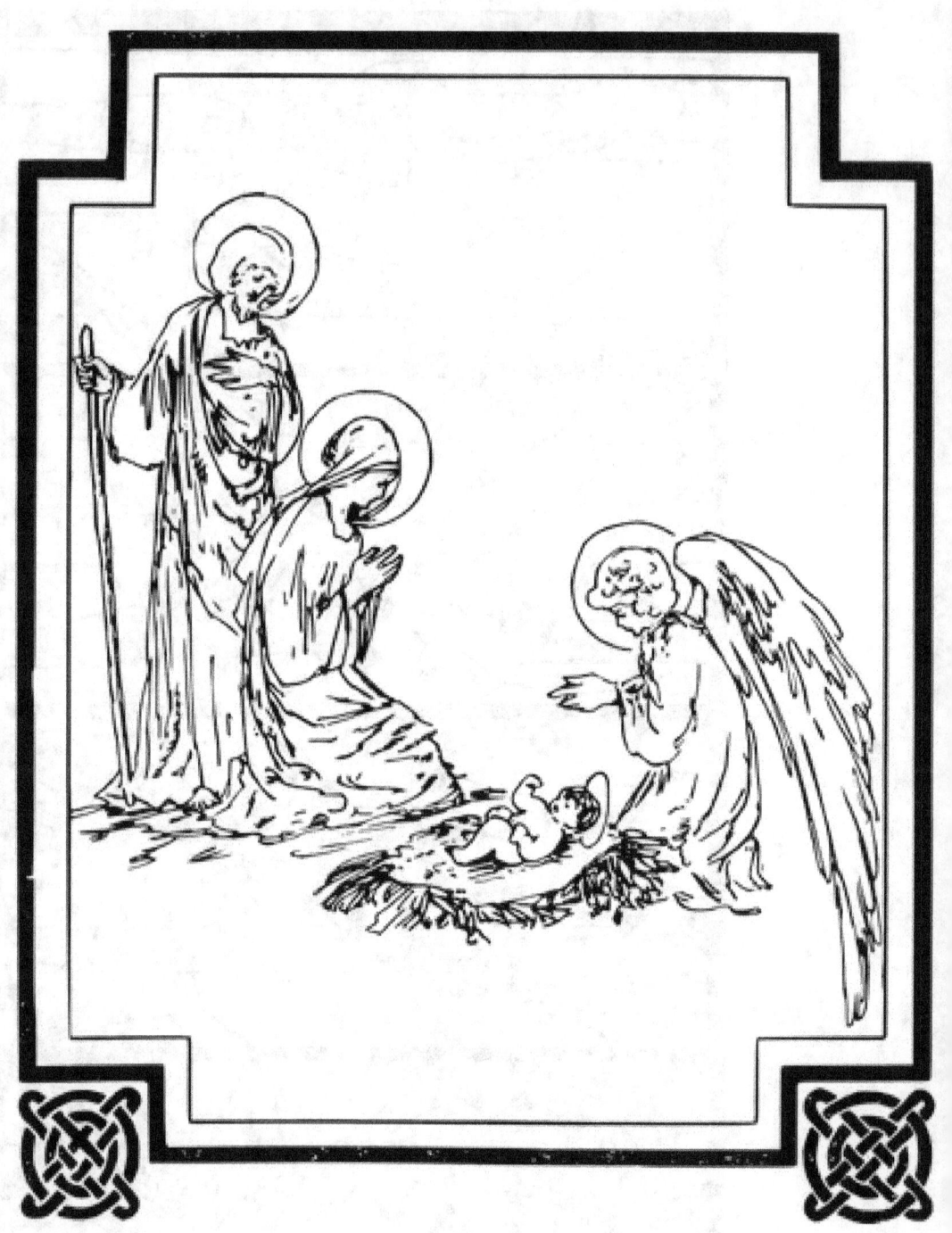

Angels Adult Coloring Book

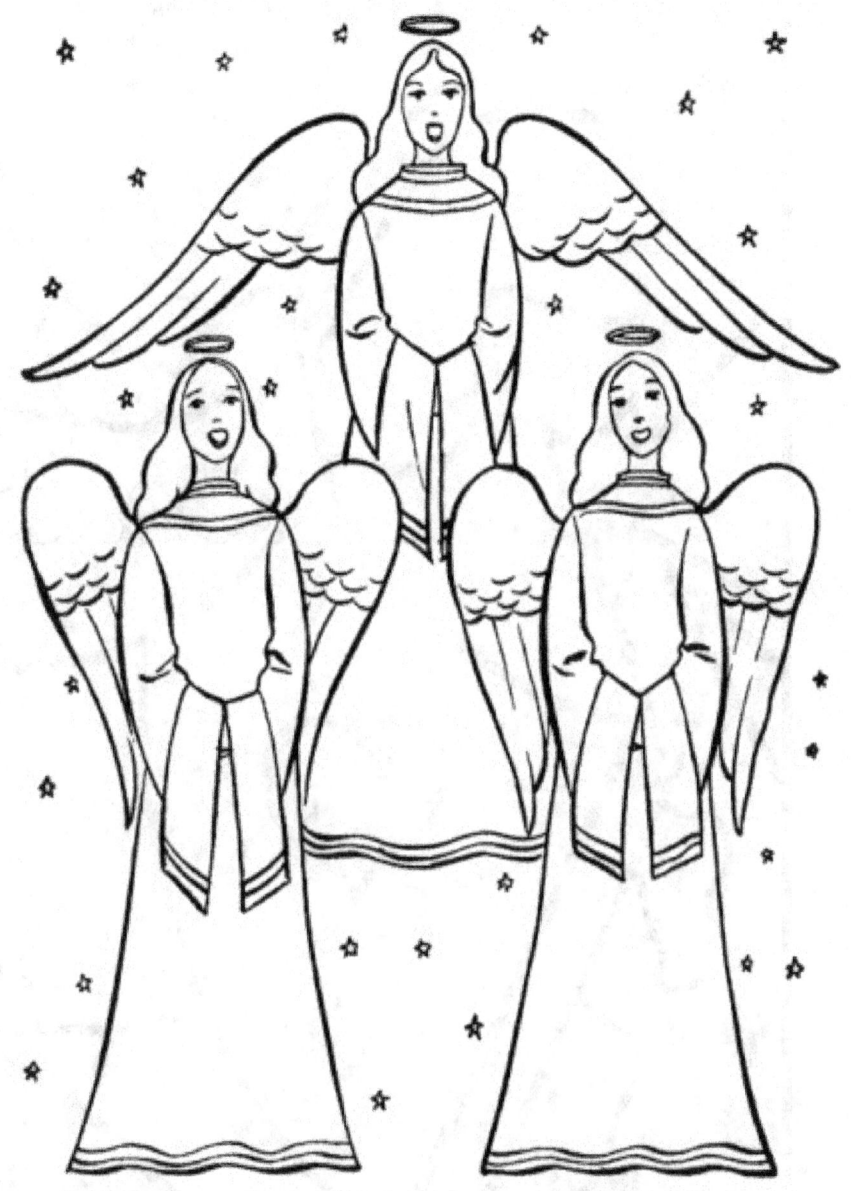

HARK THE HERALD ANGELS SING

Angels Adult Coloring Book

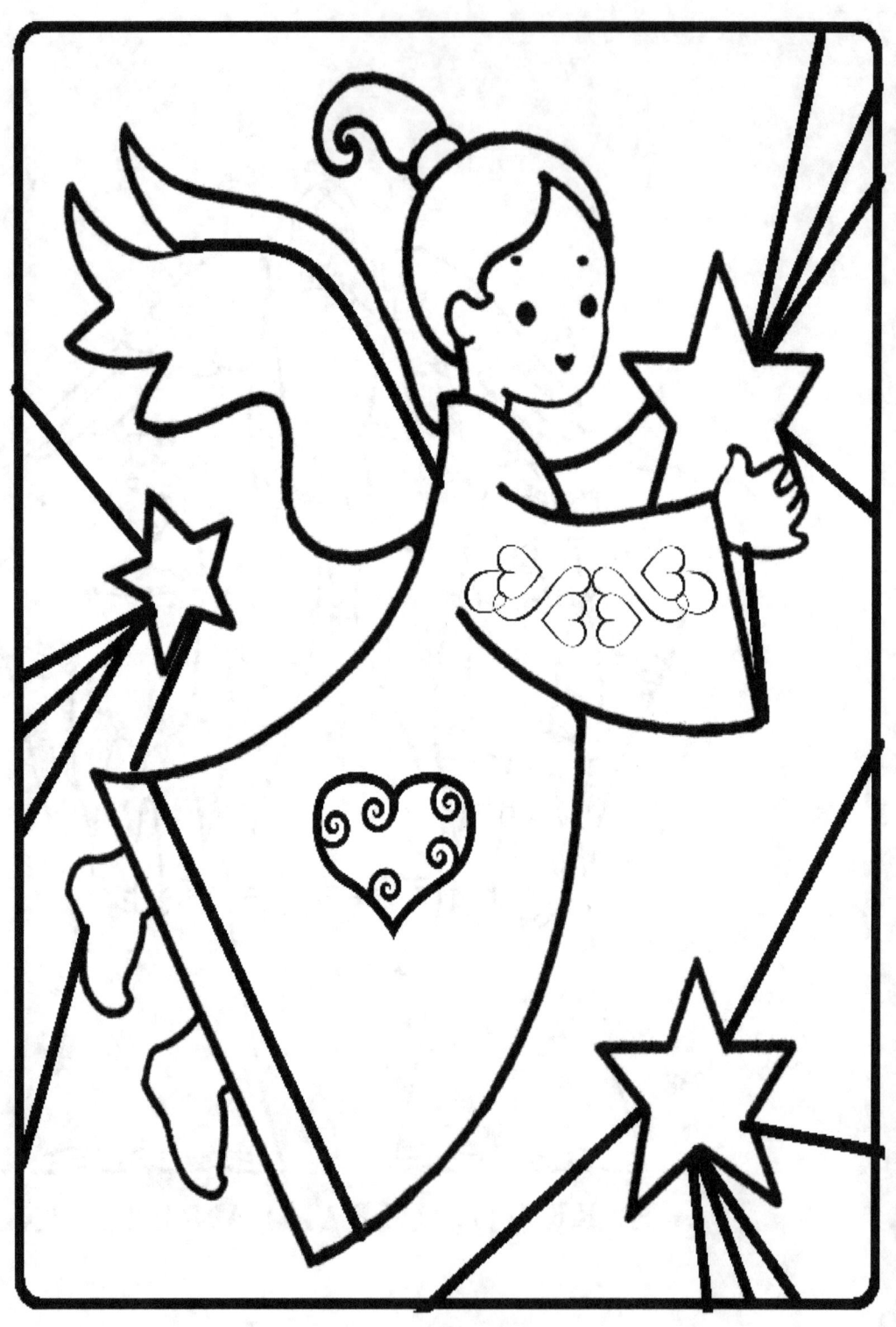

Angels Adult Coloring Book

Americana Vintage Angel

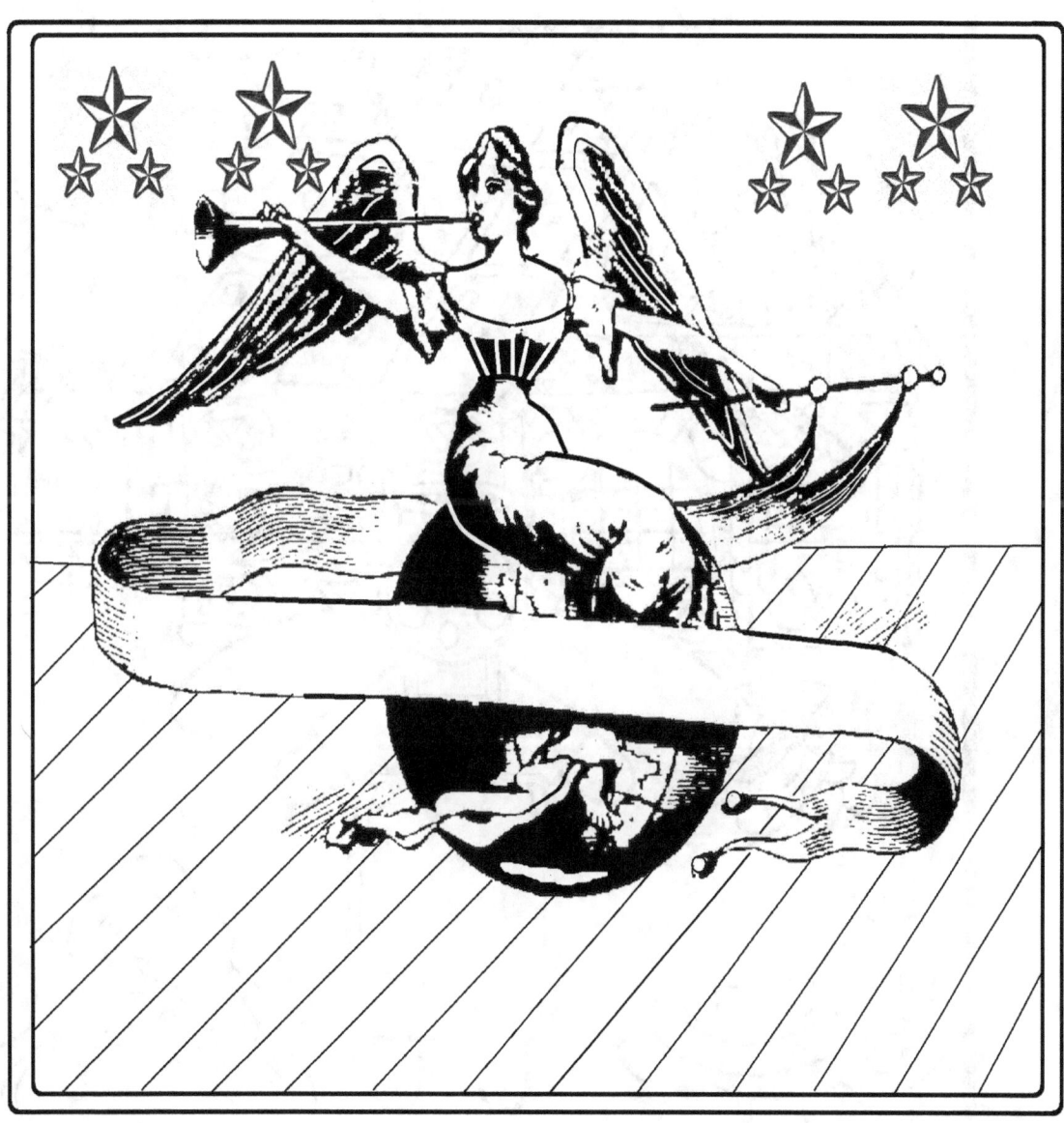

Angels Adult Coloring Book

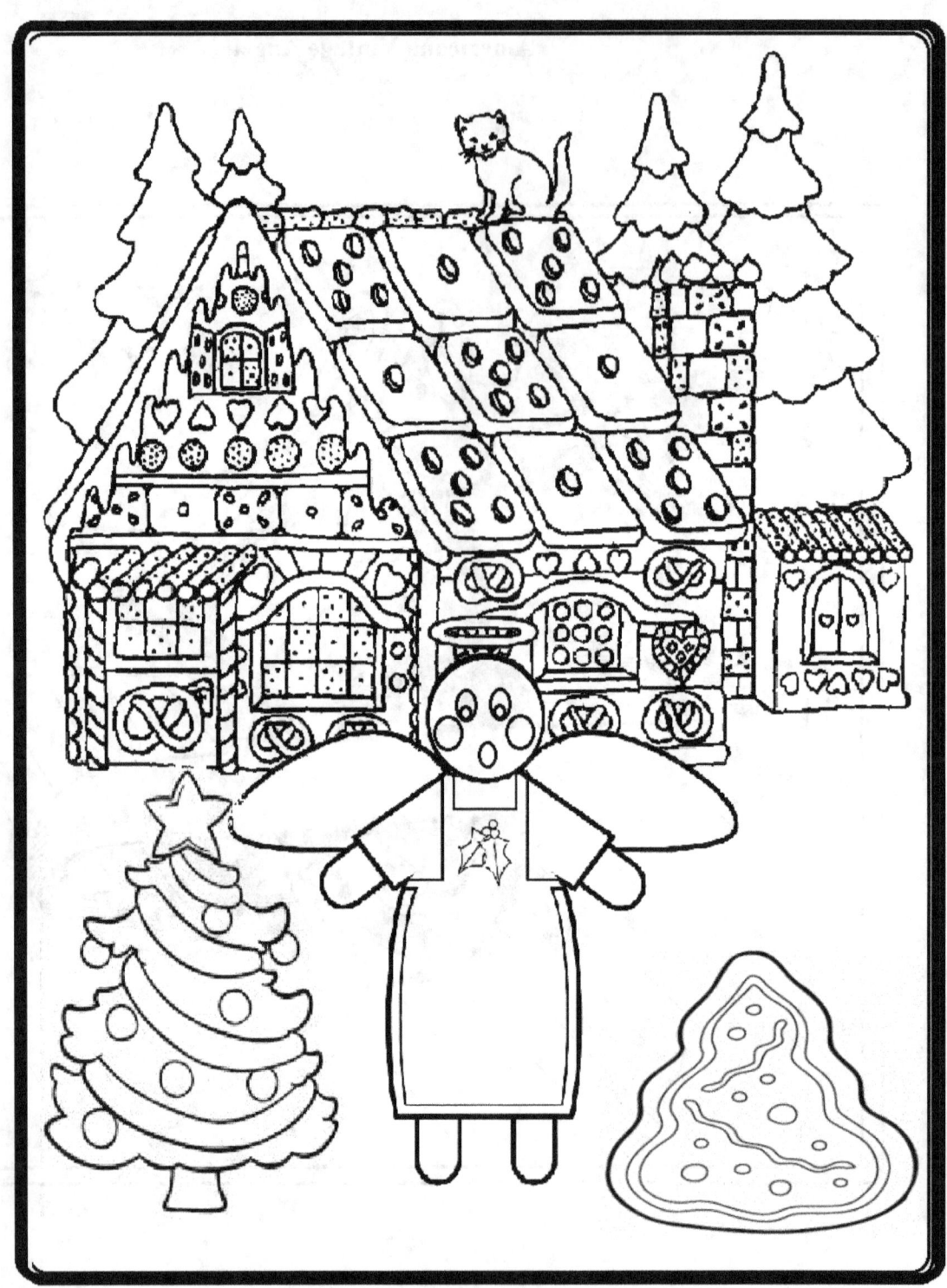

Gingerbread Angel

Angels Adult Coloring Book

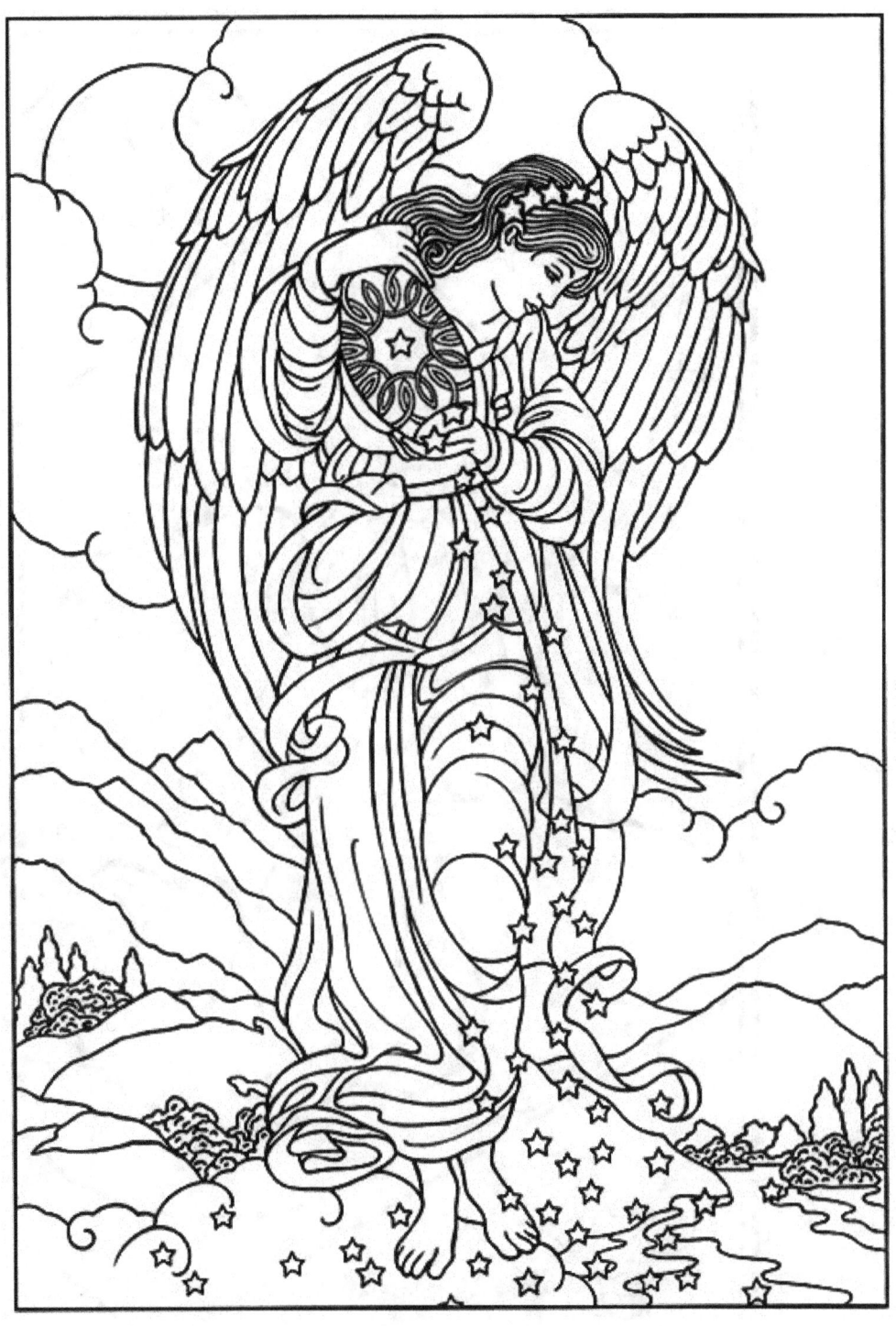

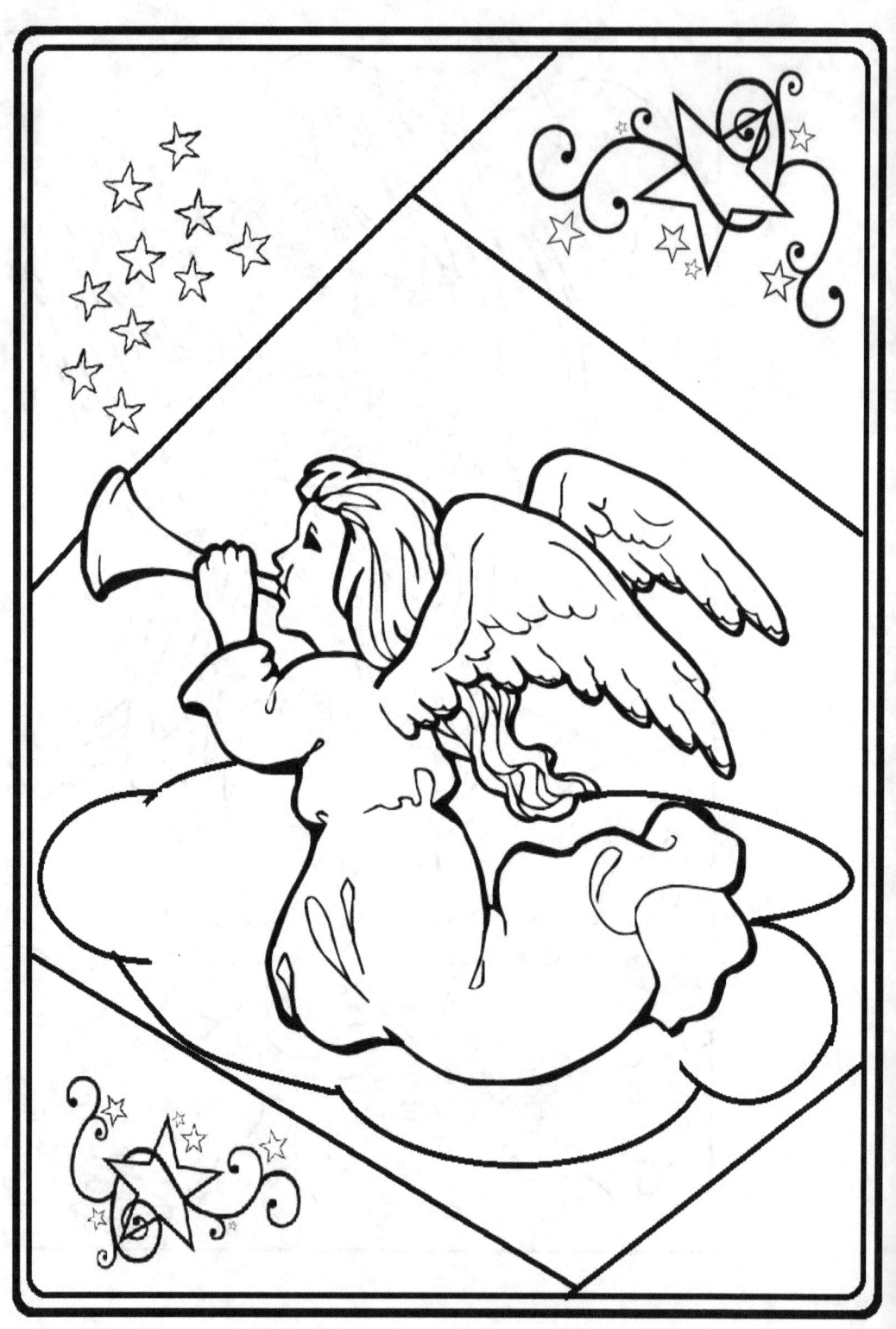

Angels Adult Coloring Book

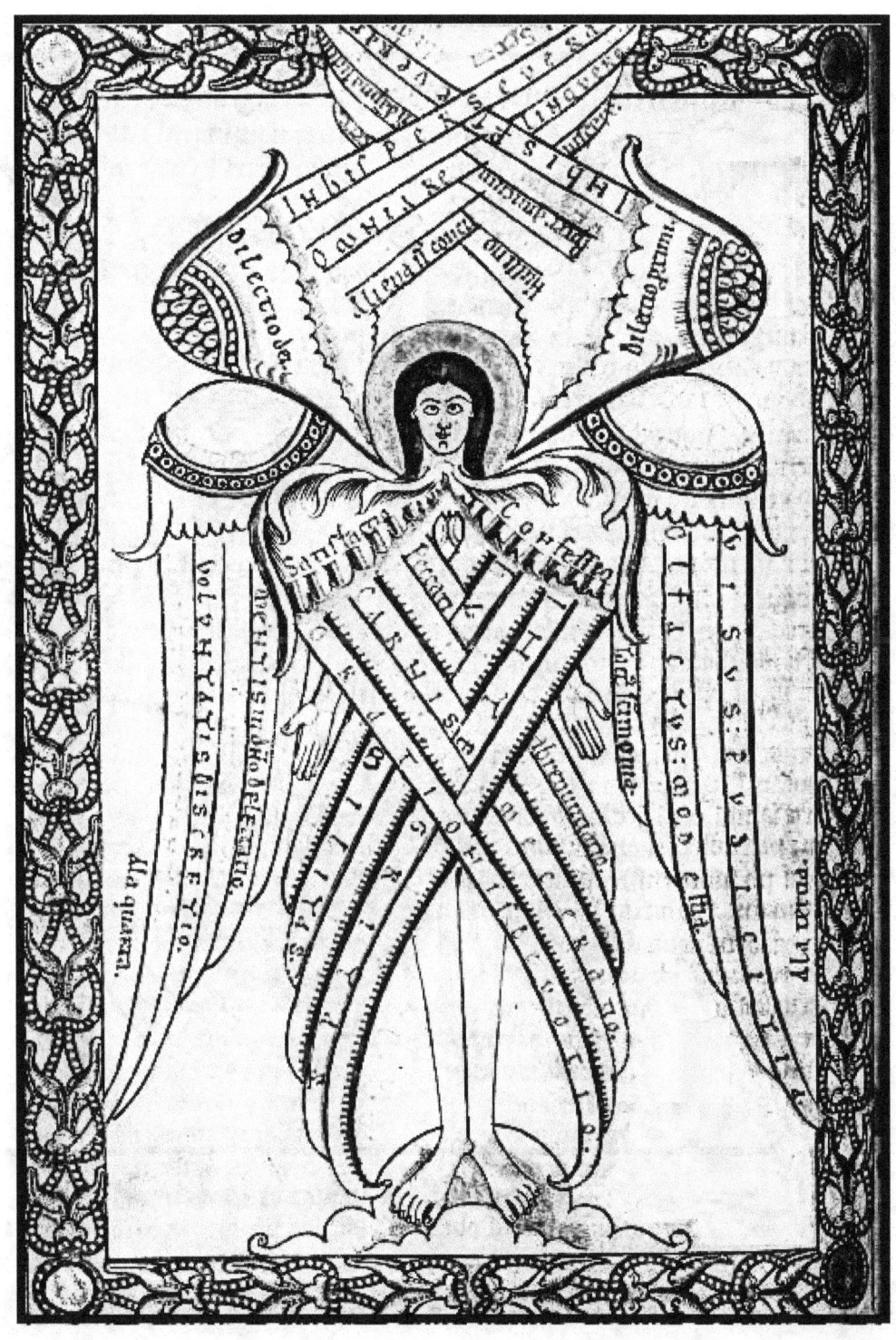

SIX-WINGED SERAPH MS 66 12TH CENTURY

Angels Adult Coloring Book

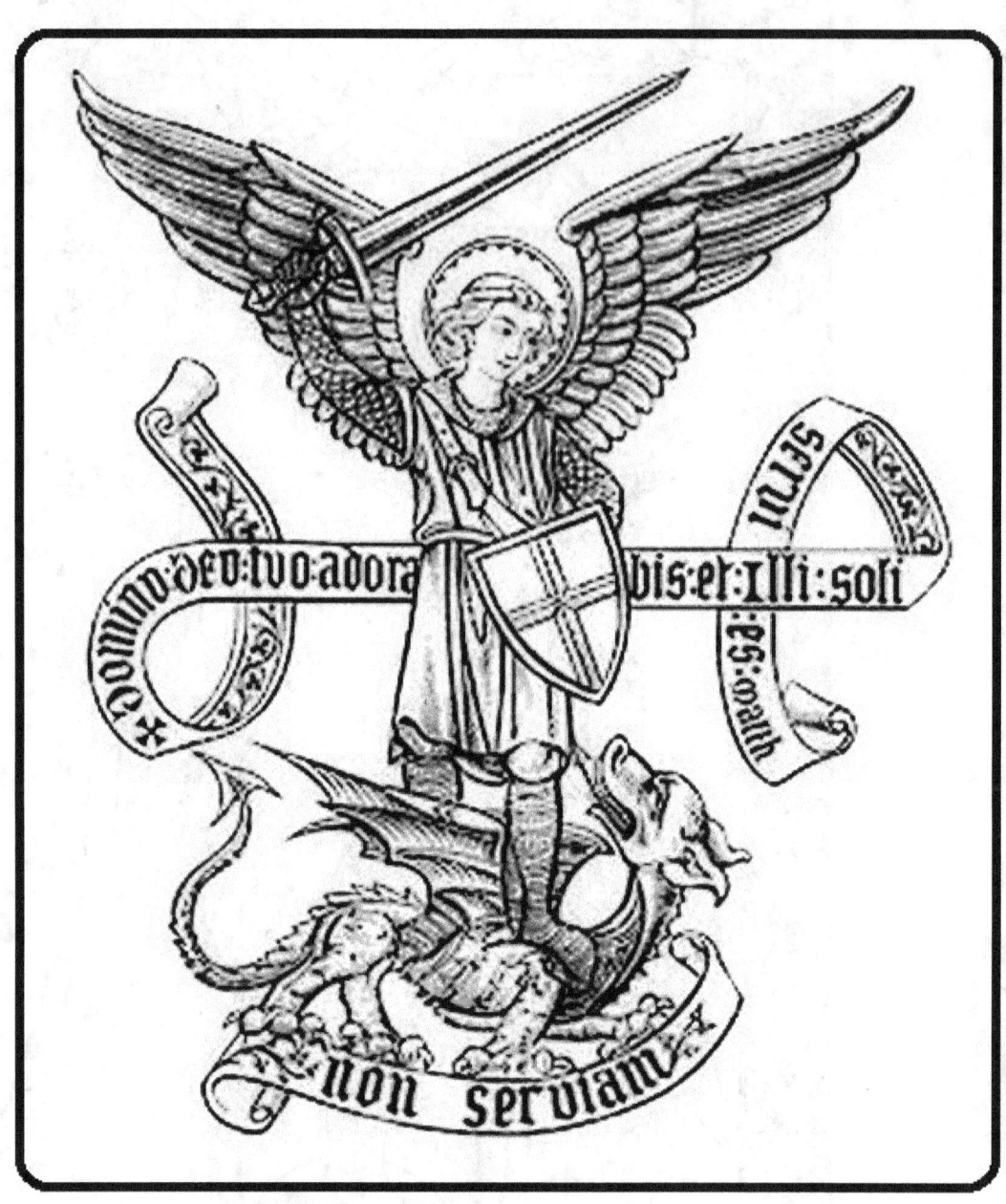

ANGEL SLAYING DRAGON

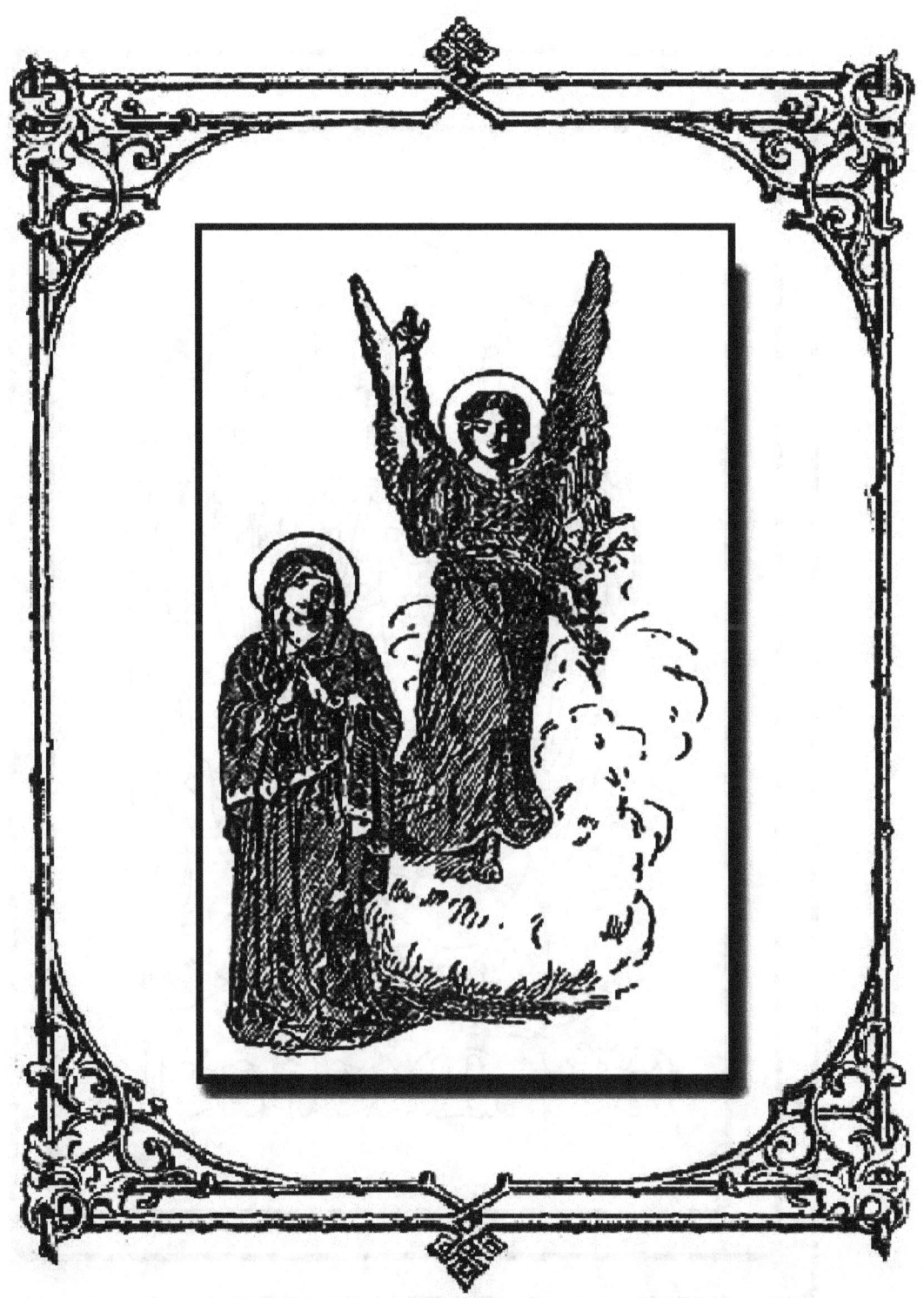

Vintage Visitation of the Angel

Angels Adult Coloring Book

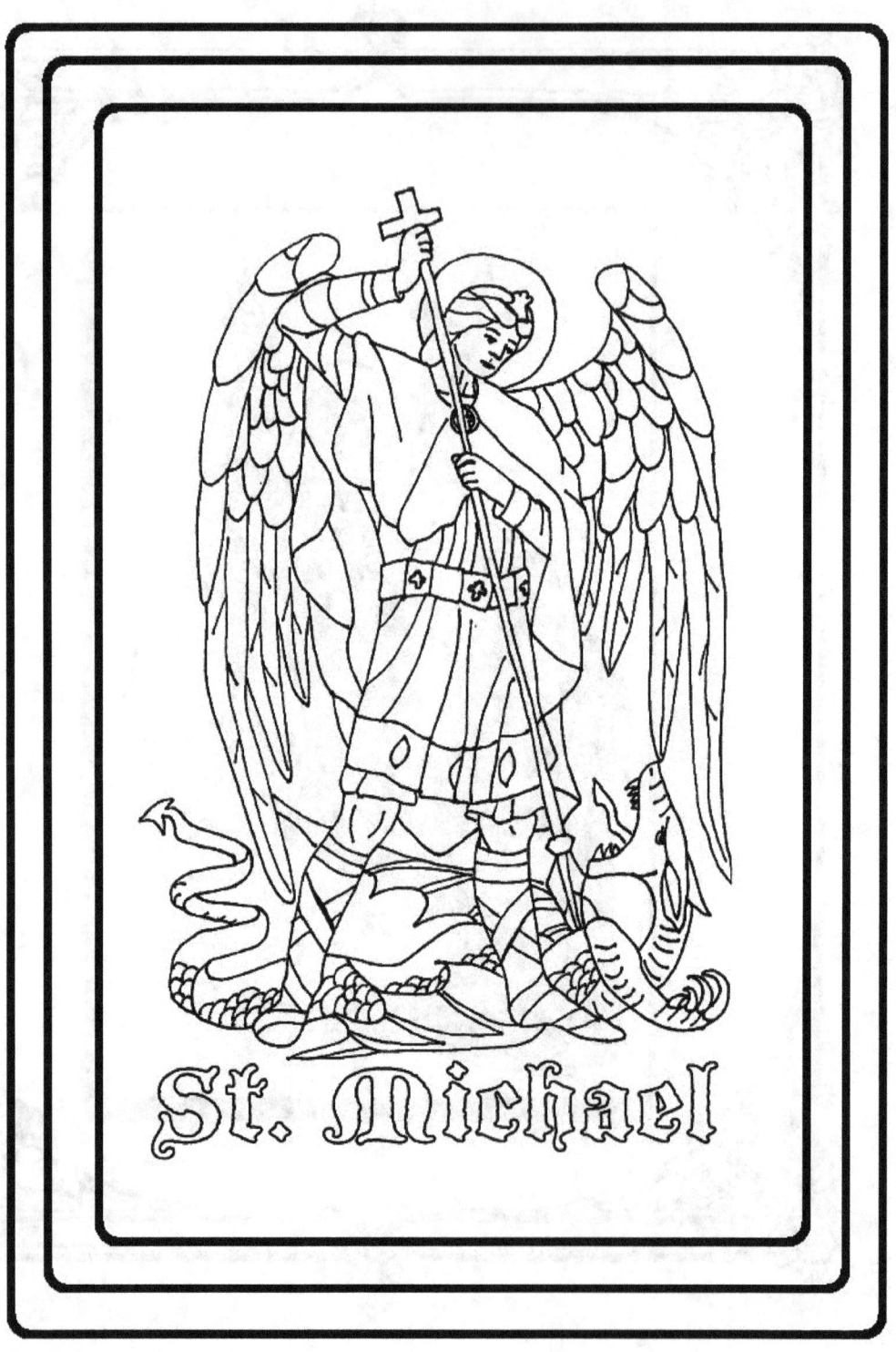

St. Michael

Angels Adult Coloring Book

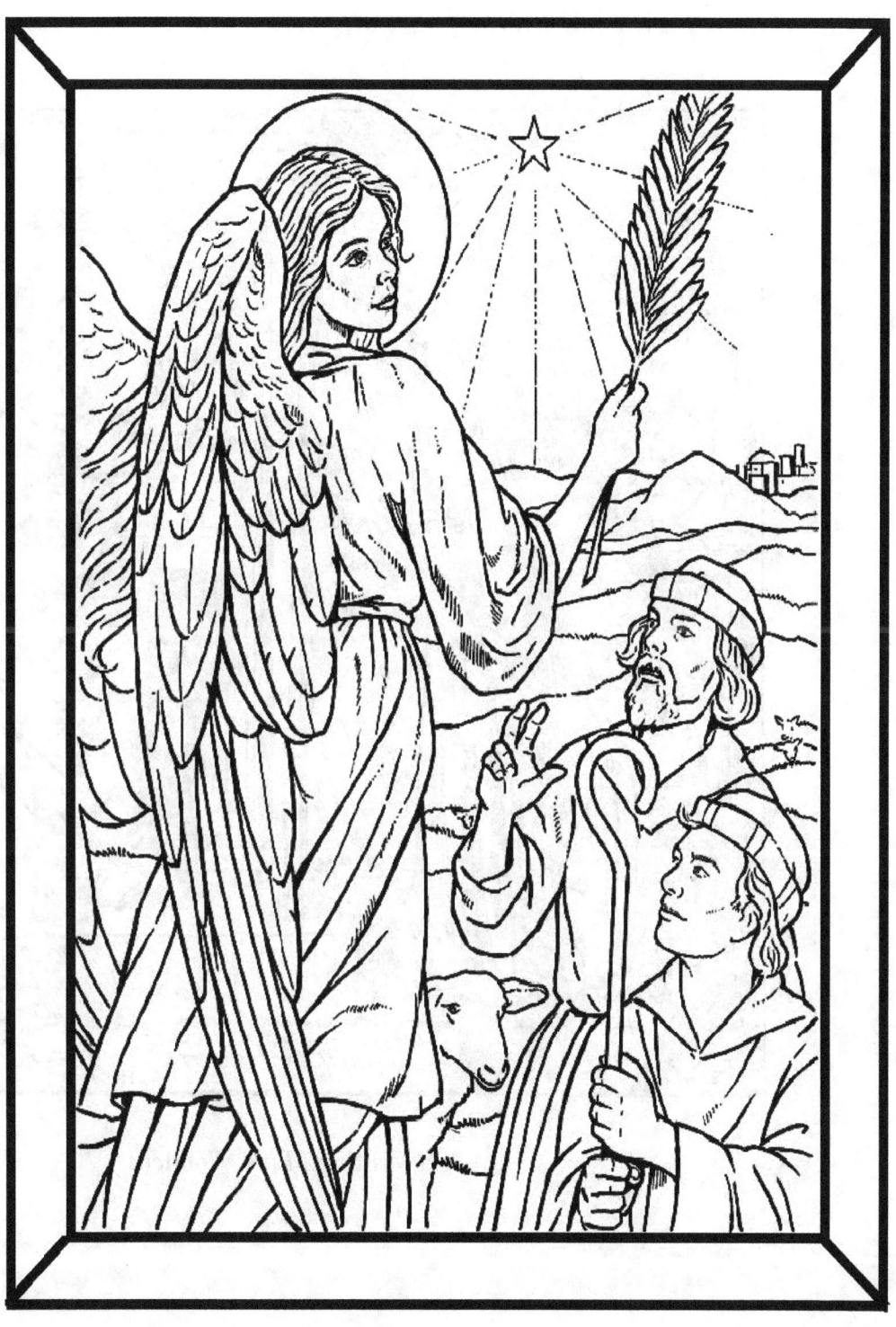

Angels Adult Coloring Book

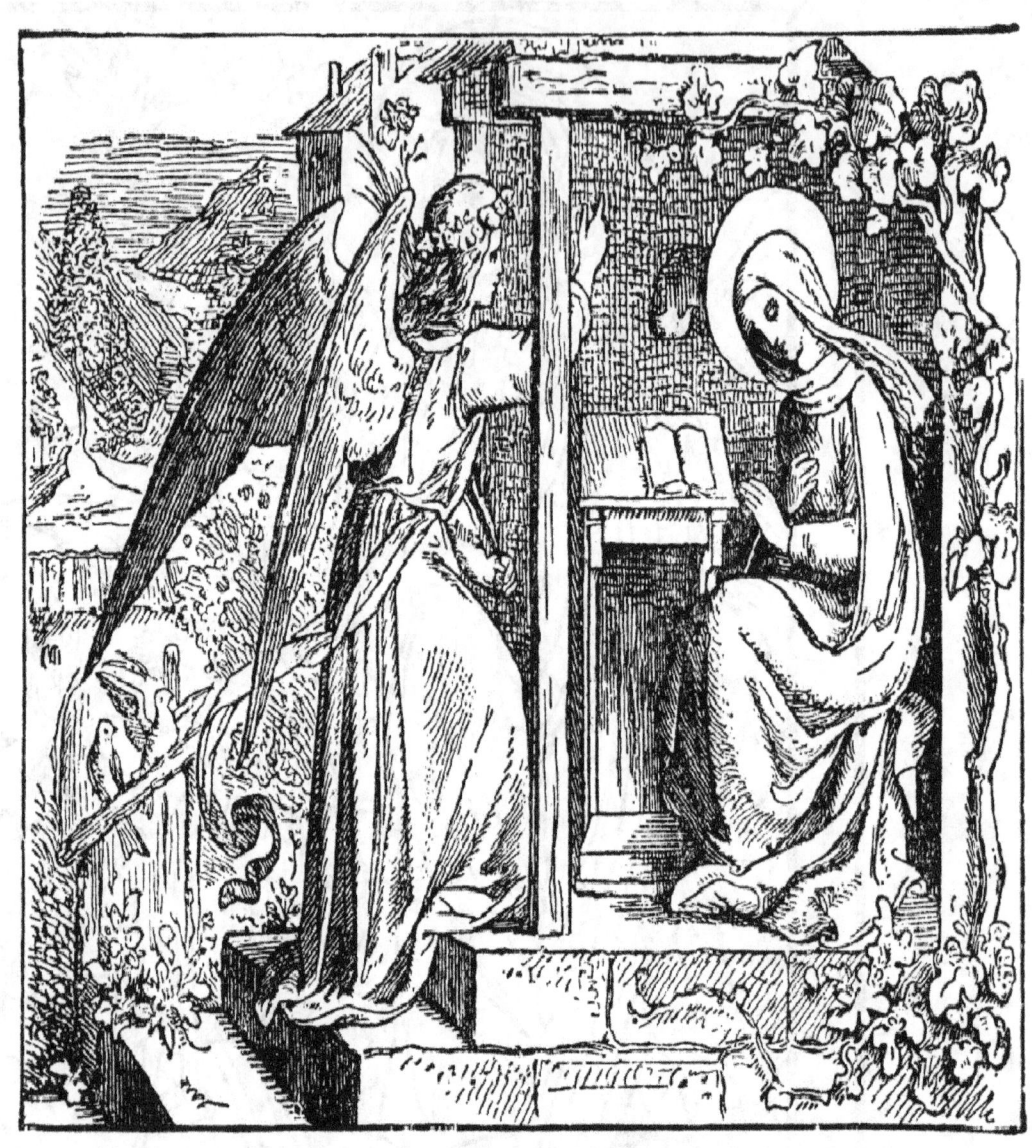

Angel Visiting Mary Woodcut

Angels Adult Coloring Book

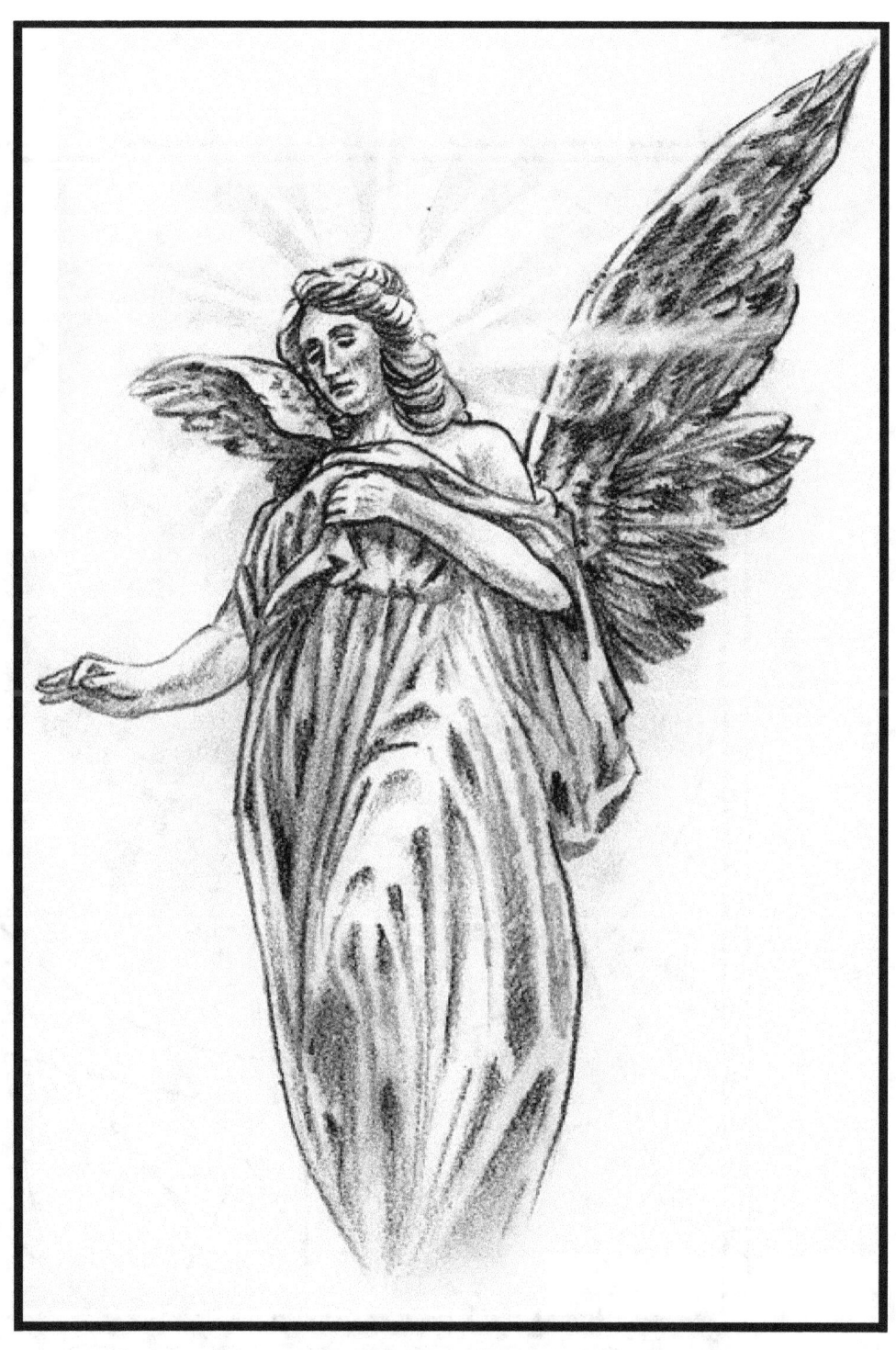

Protector Angel by freetattoodesigns.org

Angels Adult Coloring Book

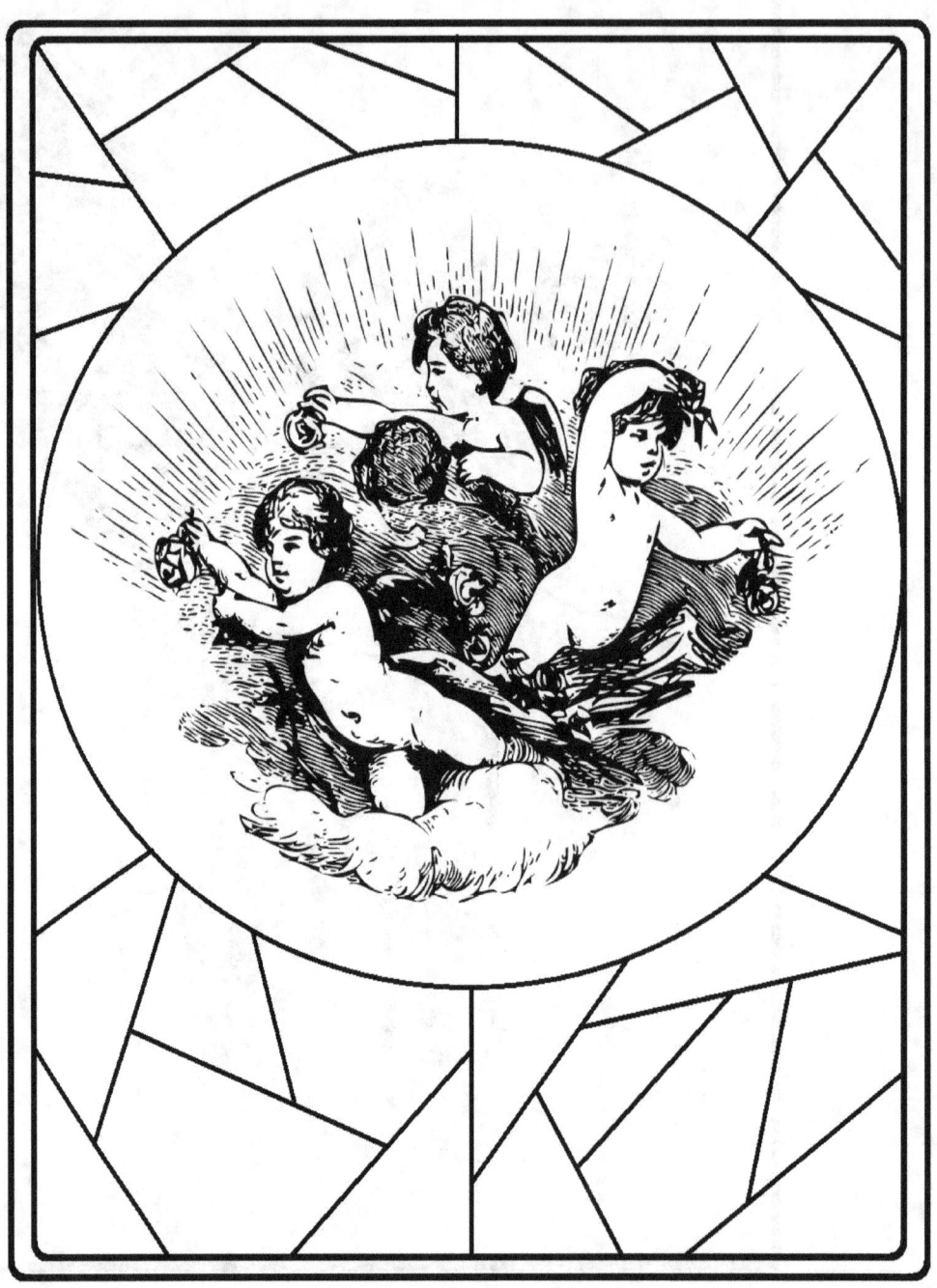

Angels Adult Coloring Book

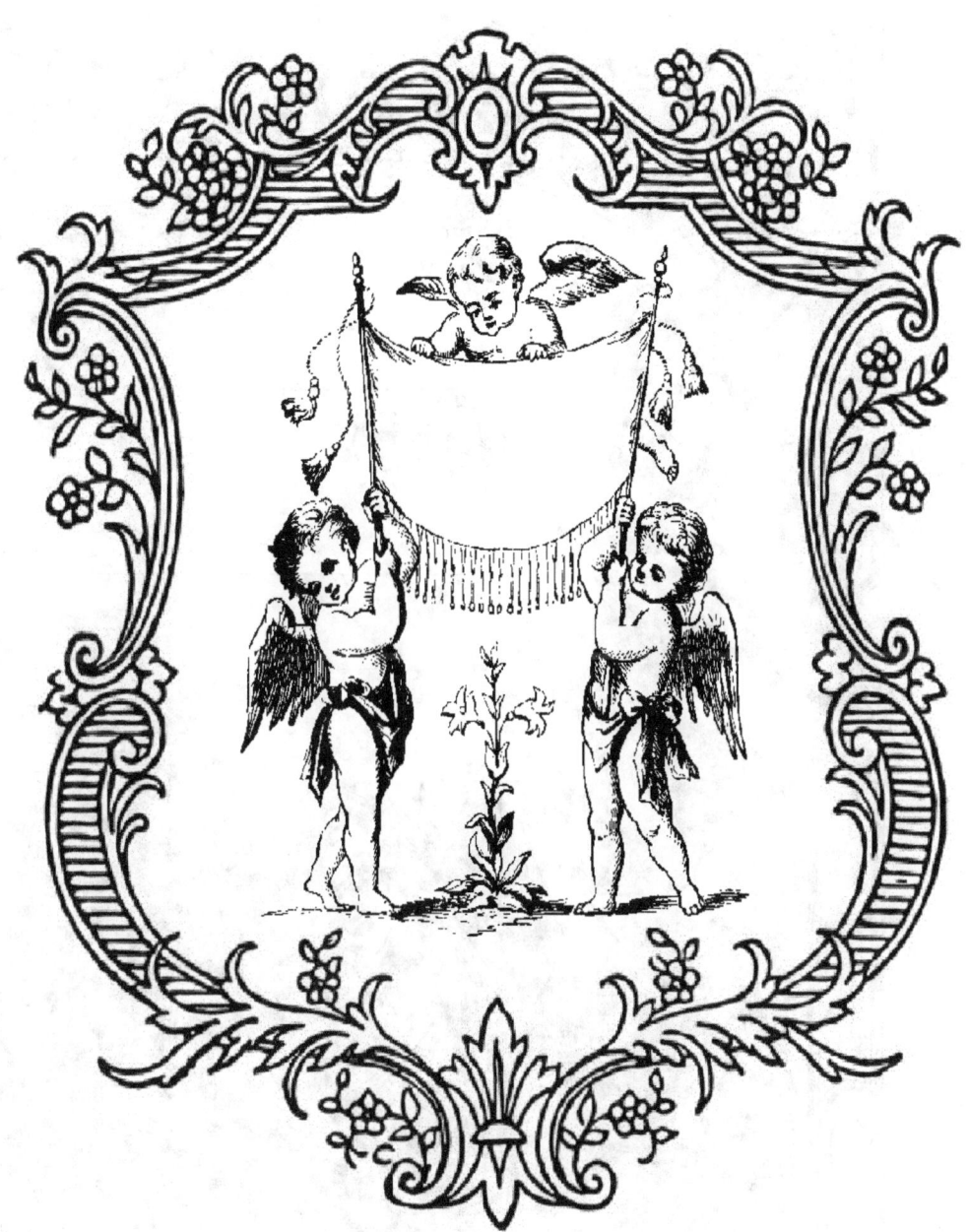

Angels Adult Coloring Book

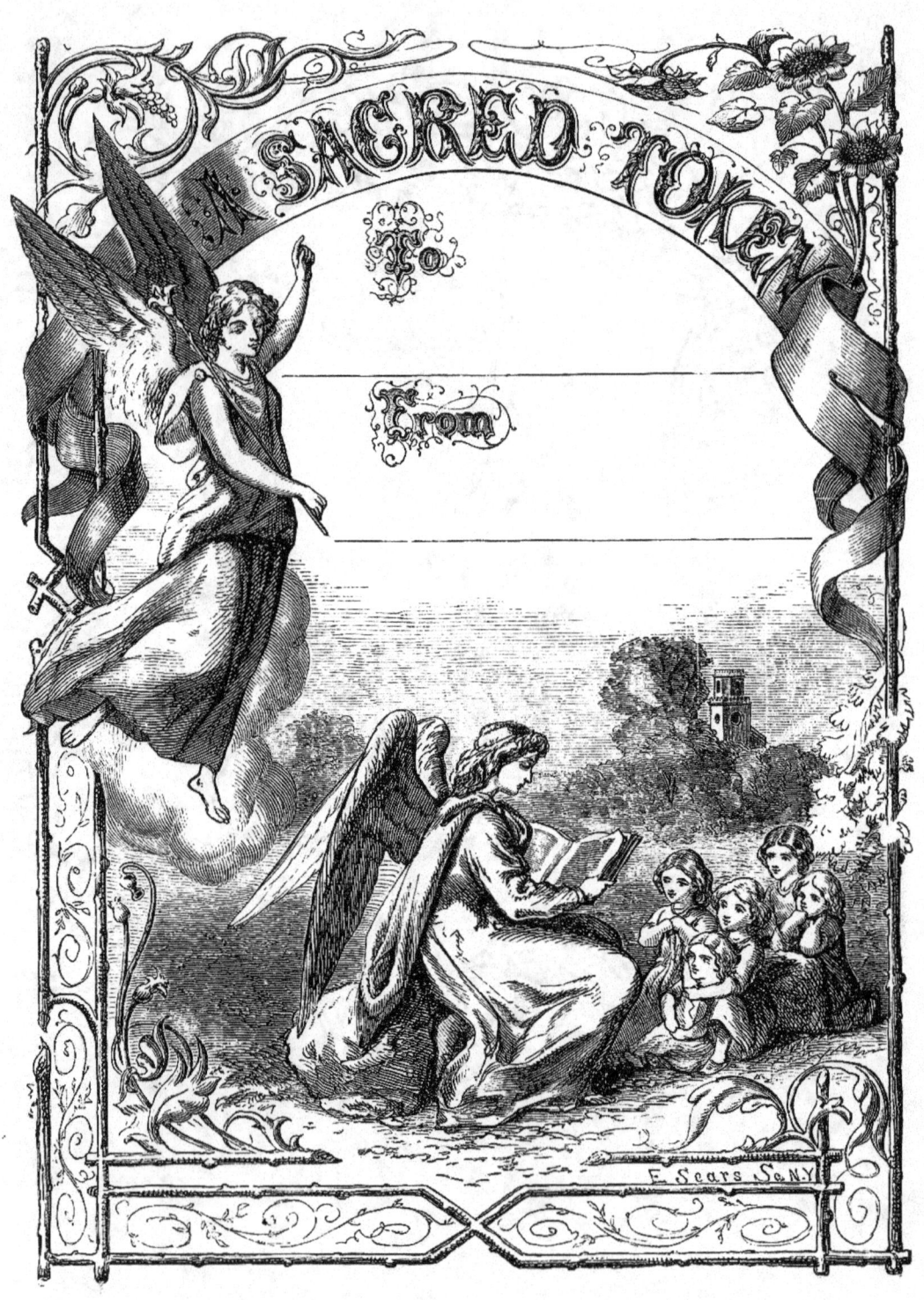

A SACRED TOKEN

To

From

E Sears Sc.N.Y

Angels Adult Coloring Book

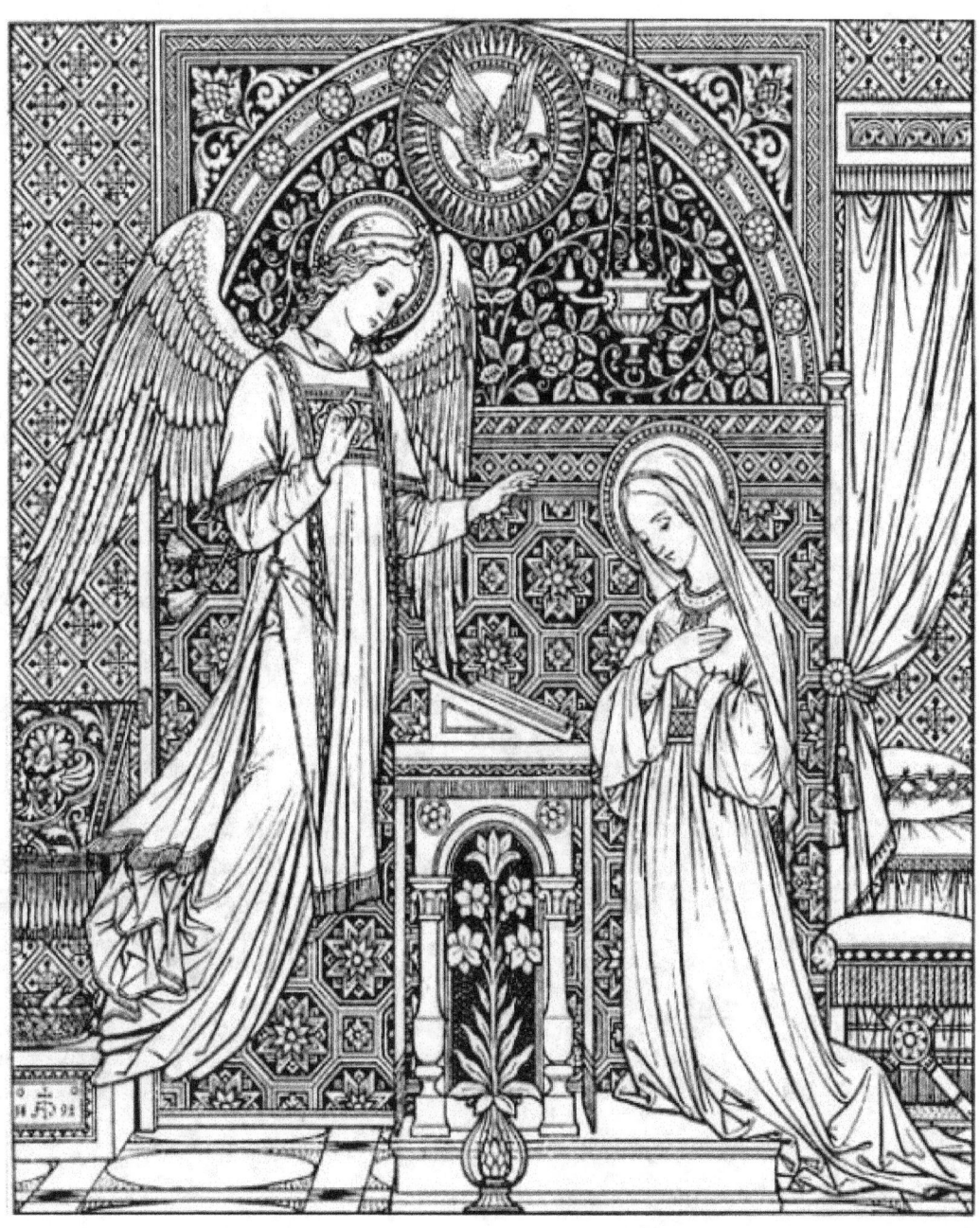

Angels Adult Coloring Book

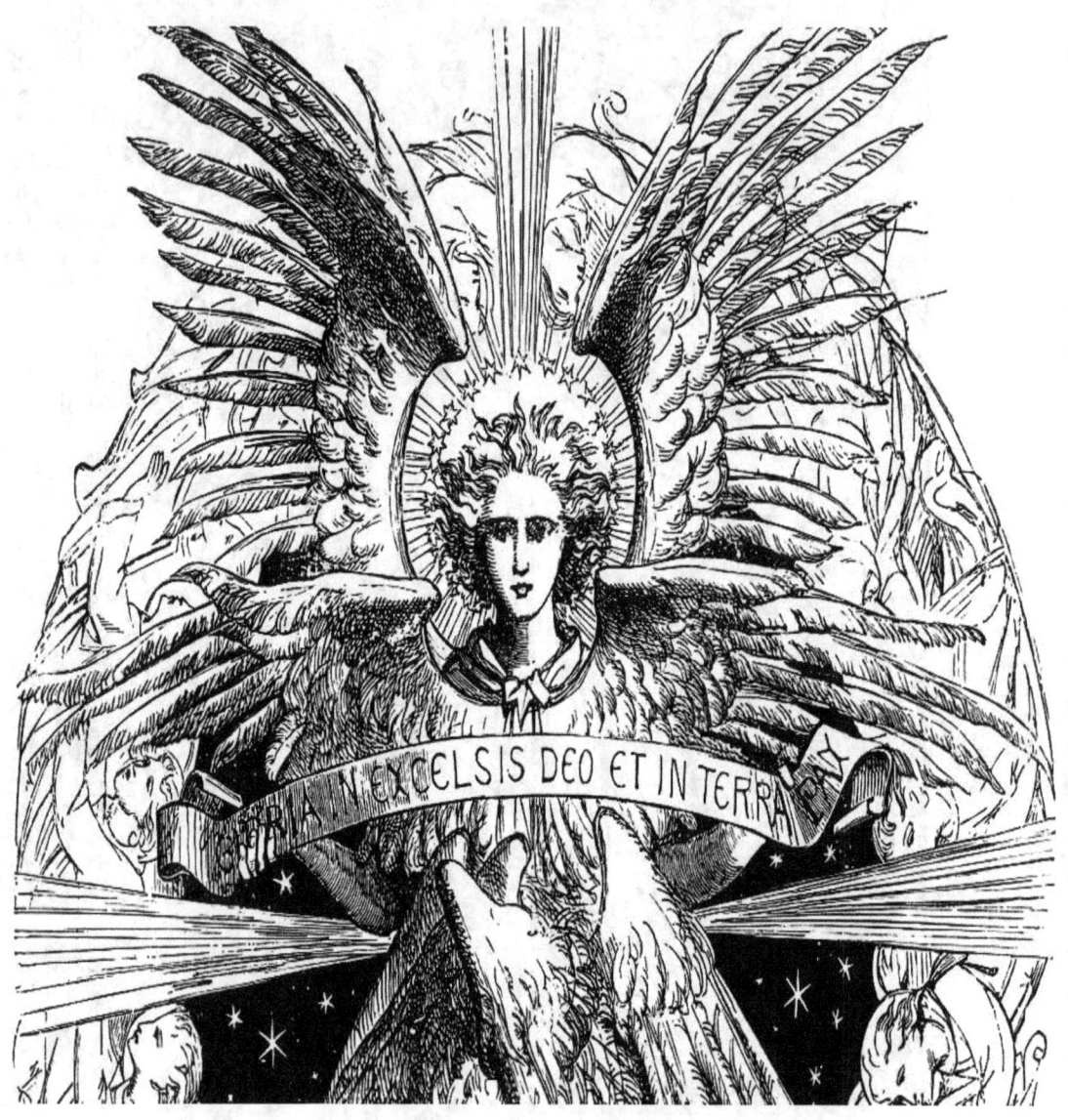

Angels Adult Coloring Book

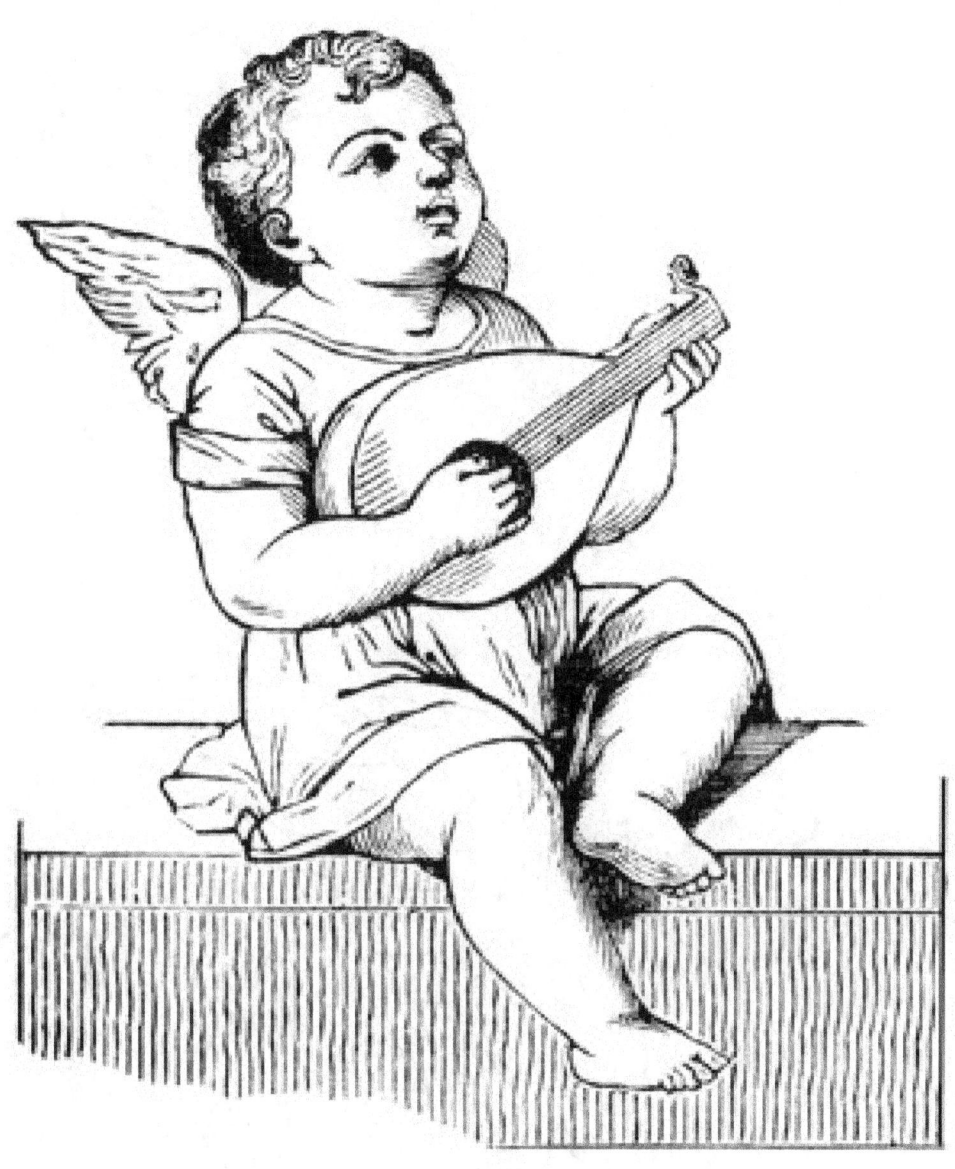

Angels Adult Coloring Book

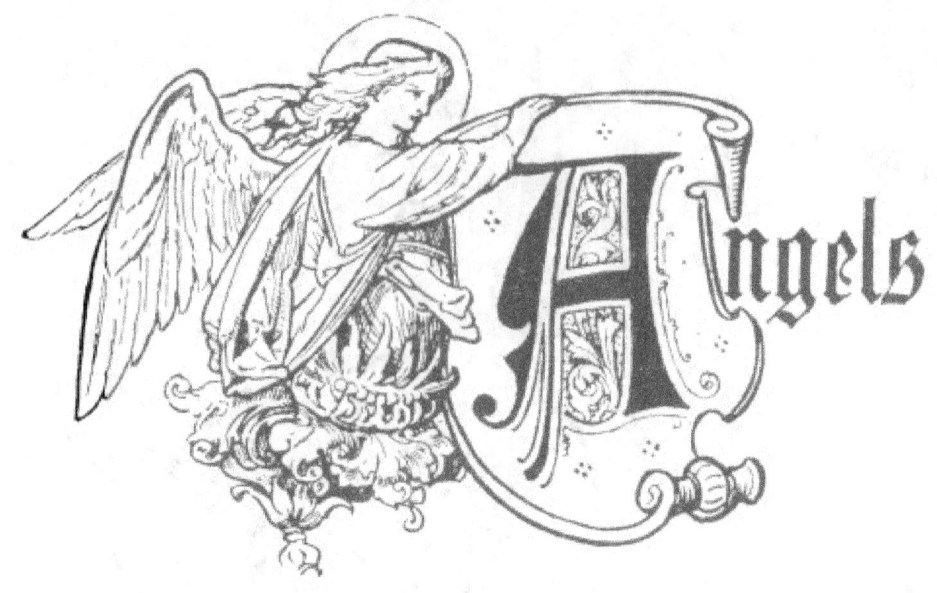

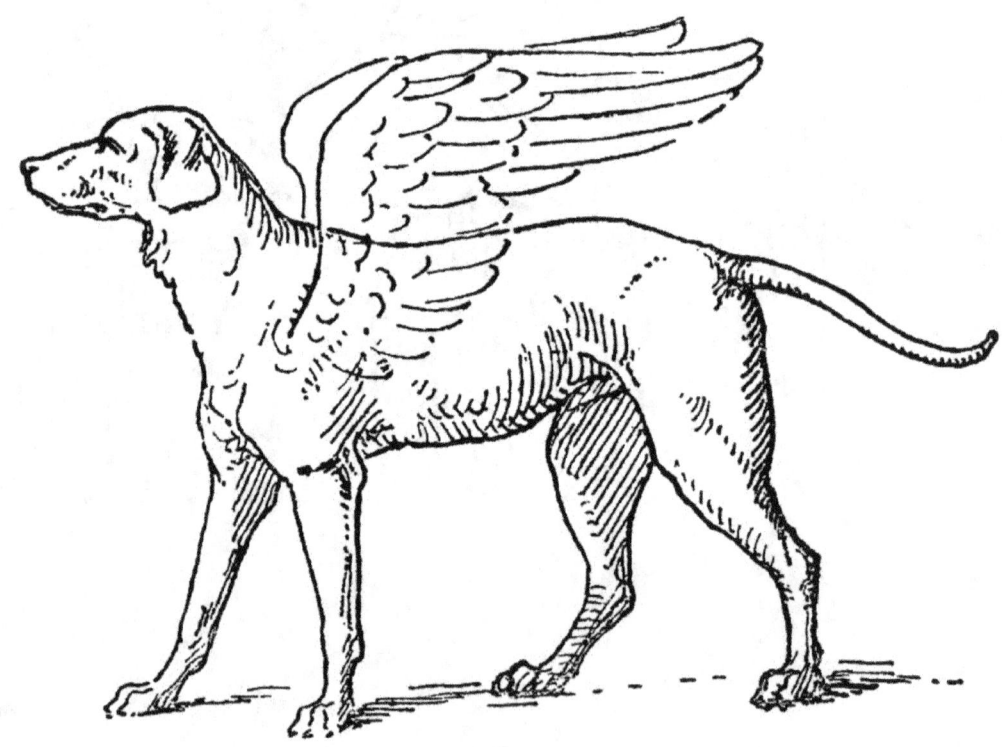

www.ingramcontent.com/pod-product-compliance
Lightning Source LLC
Chambersburg PA
CBHW081230170526
45165CB00009B/3022